Of the Greatest Generation

Ed Polokoff

1/3 / 2013

Been There, Done That,
What Now?

Been There, Done That, What Now?

Ed Polokoff

VANTAGE PRESS
New York

Excerpts are reproduced as follows:

From "The Chartist" by Edwin Polokoff. *Technical Analysis of Stocks & Commodities,* Vol. 19, No. 2 (Feb. 2001). Copyright © 2001, Technical Analysis, Inc. Used with permission.
From "Dow 1000" by Edwin Polokoff. *Technical Analysis of Stocks & Commodities,* Vol. 19, No. 10 (Oct. 2001). Copyright © 2001, Technical Analysis, Inc. Used with permission.
From "Buy High—Sell Low" by Edwin Polokoff. *Working Money*, (December 18, 2001). Copyright © 2001, Technical Analysis, Inc. Used with permission.
Charts used with permission from MC Horsey and Co., PO Box 2597, Salisbury, MD 21802, 410-742-3700.

Within this novel is a fiction novella entitled "Alex and Max."
Any similarity between the names, characters, and places in this novella
and any persons, living or dead, is purely coincidental.

Cover design by Phil Brandon

FIRST EDITION

Published by Vantage Press, Inc.
419 Park Ave. South, New York, NY 10016

Manufactured in the United States of America
ISBN: 0-533-14643-7

Library of Congress Catalog Card No.: 2003093698

0 9 8 7 6 5 4 3 2

Dedication

To Gloria and Gina, the two wives in my life.

Gloria, the gracious smiling beauty from South Bend, Indiana, and I were married in the 40s immediately following my graduation from Notre Dame Midshipmen's School. Our union produced many years of happiness plus three children, Mark, Linda, and Gail, about whom we are most proud. She was the solid mother, the anchor of stability, and the conduit of much love throughout our home. Once we started to drift apart because of contrasting personalities and goals, she had the vision to nudge me into a new phase so that I could better pursue my aspirations.

Gina, the attractive, talented goal-oriented girl from Toronto, was willing to abandon her blossoming business career in order to take a chance on a man twenty-three years her elder. Our marriage helped propel me to new heights of success and contentment. She has kept me thinking young, feeling young; she has taught me about the excitement of world travel; she has aided my business career; she beats me on the golf course; she has sparked my enthusiasm for new interests, including her work in art.

Indeed, Gloria and Gina have given me two bull markets in marriage, for which I am grateful. There is no rancor in our family stemming from a model divorce. My children and six grandchildren are relaxed about our relationships.

I am a lucky guy.

Contents

Foreword

In my next life—and there will be one, right?—I would like to be a writer or a jazz musician. The more I thought about it, the more I decided that I better not take any chances on the hereafter. Why not be a writer now? I can work on the musician part later.

I have no complaints about what I have done or enjoyed so far. There was the boyhood in sleepy Poughkeepsie, New York, the stint at Duke University, the growing into manhood odyssey during the "good war" as a naval officer in the South Pacific.

I accepted the only job offer I received after the war as an instructor at the University of Buffalo where I taught economics to mostly World War II veterans. Then came the life at Merrill Lynch as a broker and money manager for fifty consecutive years—some kind of record at my firm. At my retirement party in New York City hosted by the Chairman of the Board and attended by many prominent Merrill Lynchers, I was feted as a legend—a nice way to go out.

These days, in addition to playing golf, traveling, watching after the family finances while contending with the markets, keeping up with the piano, I have been doing some writing for family and friends. In my days with Merrill, I wrote market letters for clients. To date, I have completed about twenty-five works on assorted subjects. Three were published by *Stocks and Commodities*, a magazine dealing with financial matters. Several others were rejected by magazines.

I have no illusions about becoming a prominent author. Many have encouraged me to embark on this writing adventure because they think readers will like my pieces.

I hope you do.

Acknowledgments

The words are mine, but there is a little bit of many people in this book.

Without my wife, Gina, who guided me on the ABC's of the computer, this writing effort would have extended into many extra months. More importantly, she and I enjoyed lengthy discussions during our four-mile walks three times weekly, and her input helped me in the recall process and in the consolidation of diverse thoughts.

My children, Mark, Linda, and Gail and my grandchildren, refreshed me with extensive tidbits of information. Son-in-law Phil Brandon, a talented artist and advertising executive, designed the cover.

After retirement, I attended writer's classes and workshops at Duke University, the University of Buffalo, Key West, and Florida Atlantic University. Teacher Barbara Schwartz, and students, Bob Born, Lisa Decker, Bob Freeman, and particularly, Nancy Pateman, sparked my desire to get into writing in my very first class at FAU.

There were friends such as Scott Umstead, Harvey Frumkin, Del Dunghe, John Ting and many at Boca Grove Country Club who critiqued and encouraged my essays. This project of writing these pieces has been a stimulating part of my retirement experience.

I

About the Stock Market

The Chartist

I shall never forget George.

A man in his late fifties, somewhat paunchy but not fat, medium height, dark hair streaked with gray, silver-rimmed glasses shielding tired eyes, George looked docile. A closer look betrayed his seemingly easygoing manner. His hands shook slightly but uncontrollably, especially when he ate or wrote. My conclusion was that he had been through too many stock market wars, and the wear and tear on his nerves had created the nerve problem. No, probably not Parkinson's. Just stress from his occupation.

George was a professional speculator, a broker with one account, the family account. He lived on the edge of great wealth or imminent poverty. His patrician bearing was suggestive of good breeding, a Park Avenue childhood. How surprised his acquaintances at the country club would have been if they had known that this quiet, solicitous man, who could pass for a philosophy instructor at the university, could be such a ferocious gambler.

In those early days of the 1950s, since I often worked at the office every late afternoon doing my research and planning, I became more familiar with George and his theories and modus operandi. With the office mostly deserted by that time of the day, George would occasionally break the silence and chat with me. Lecture me on his techniques. I can still see his figure hunched over the desk, his meticulous, patterned routine of making penciled entries on each of his about 100 separate pages of charts in a big binder. Yes, George was a chartist. The charts were his bible; no need to know economics or business or financial analysis. He would say that the chart on each security he followed was the com-

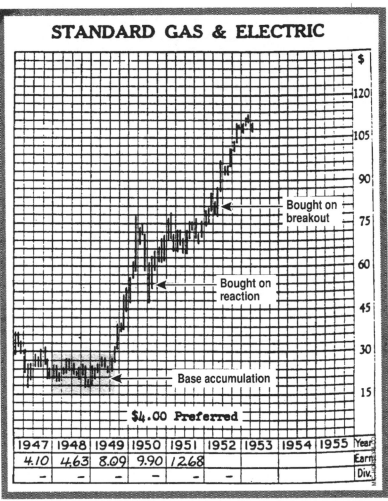

FIGURE 1: STANDARD GAS & ELECTRIC. George the chartist paid no attention to the talk about this company, instead following its movements and buying it when his technique indicated he should.

posite of all of the thinking and information available. Chart skill involved interpreting the hieroglyphics in order to discover investment opportunities.

Oh, I will not burden you with George's attempts to teach me. I will tell you that much of his theory made sense, that he was very adept at his craft, but that I trusted fundamental analysis over chart interpretations. And when George would say to me, "I know nothing about the stock market or about individual companies, but my charts know everything," I would smile. Was George serious or was he pulling my leg?

I eventually learned that he had once owned a seat on the New York Stock Exchange, had made a fortune, and then lost it in the 1929 break. I wished so much that he would make one more big hit in order to restore his financial health. I did not want him to live the rest of his life trading stocks in order to make a living. Maybe the shaking would stop if he could retire with a decent stake.

One afternoon, about 5:00 P.M., George sauntered back to my desk where I was deeply engrossed in trying to decide whether I would be recommending a specific stock for my clients.

"Excuse me for bothering you, Eddy. But I own a stock that might interest you. I started buying it a few years ago around eighteen dollars when it broke out of its base. I've added to my holdings over a period of time, and I have quite a big position, even though I know nothing about it."

"Come on, George," I smiled. "You know nothing about it. Are you kidding me?" He occasionally feigned stupidity, and I was never able to figure out whether he was serious or not.

"No. I'm not kidding. Would you check it out and tell me what you think I should do with it. You seem to be a bright young guy."

"What's it called?"

With a straight face, George replied, "SG $4 pr. Whatever that stands for."

"You don't know the name of the company?"

"Eddy, what difference would it make? I don't know anything

5

about stocks or the market. I just know charts."

I checked the quotation book, the *Standard and Poor* manual, studied briefly the information about the security and replied, "Standard Gas and Electric $4 preferred is the name of the issue. In the reorganization of the company after it had gone bankrupt in the 30s, this particular stock was accorded no value. It is worthless. I'd sell it."

George stared at me with that plaintive look. There was a long pause.

"Eddy, it's up quite a bit since I first bought it. It sells around fifty dollars now. It has had its first reaction in a while, and the chart pattern looks wonderful. I'm thinking of buying more on this dip."

"But the court ruled that it has no value."

"Thank you, I still might buy some more."

George kept me and a few other colleagues apprised of his additional purchases in spite of our protestations. We sincerely worried about his fixation with this idea, and we were concerned that the eventual collapse (and it would collapse, right?) in the price of the stock would be devastating to his physical and mental health.

One wintry day, we cajoled George into joining us for coffee in a restaurant across from the office. The scene was almost comic: the four of us brokers, the top people in the office, were huddled around our friend at the table, imploring him to cash his profits,which had become substantial and enjoy the bonanza he had gained. He resisted our pleas stubbornly.

"Someone knows more than we do about this stock. The chart picture tells me to buy more."

We retorted, "George, it's a 'short squeeze.' It's an artificial price. Those who sold the stock short, expecting the price to decline, are being frightened into buying back their shares. That's why it is going up."

"I'm sorry. I'm buying more stock tomorrow morning. It has resumed its uptrend. You should think about buying a few shares for yourself and your clients."

I almost laughed!

The price was over seventy dollars.

We gave up. Let the dumb, crazy S.O.B. try to live out his fantasy. Let him lose his money. We had done all we could do to steer him right.

Over a period of time, George had accumulated about 100,000 shares of SG $4 pr, and he owned it on margin (using borrowed money to pyramid his holdings). How could he sleep owning such a position?

A few weeks later, a short article appeared in the *Wall Street Journal* in an inconspicuous space away from all the important news in the paper. It was a four- or five-paragraph story about the Standard Gas & Electric Company. A judge had ruled that under the terms of the reorganization of the formerly bankrupt company, the holders of the Standard Gas $4 preferred stock were unfairly treated, and in the revised reorganization, holders of these shares could exchange each hundred shares for shares of DQE (an electric utility) worth about a hundred and ten dollars.

We were stunned, but jubilant. George had pulled off an incredible coup, and we had witnessed the event as it unfolded before our eyes.

There was celebration in the office, and we "experts" felt rather stupid. George grinned sheepishly and accepted our congratulations graciously.

His ship had come in; he was wealthy again. He took no credit for his success.

"The charts don't lie, fellows. The charts told me something was going on. I'm sorry you didn't follow my advice."

This all happened in the 50s—so long ago that I'm amazed that I can still recall the story so vividly. I also remember how I fretted restlessly in my sleep for several nights with the thought: "Eddy, you blew it. You could have become a hero if you had bought Standard Gas $4 pr for your clients. You could have jump-started your young career to immediate stardom. New clients would have been

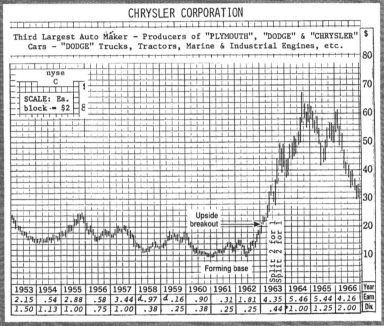

CHRYSLER CORPORATION

Third Largest Auto Maker – Producers of "PLYMOUTH", "DODGE" & "CHRYSLER"
Cars – "DODGE" Trucks, Tractors, Marine & Industrial Engines, etc.

nyse
C

SCALE: Ea.
block = $2

Upside
breakout

Split 2 for 1
Split 2 for 1

Forming base

Year	1953	1954	1955	1956	1957	1958	1959	1960	1961	1962	1963	1964	1965	1966
Earn	2.15	.54	2.88	.58	3.44	d.97	d.16	.90	.31	1.81	4.35	5.46	5.44	4.16
Div.	1.50	1.13	1.00	.75	1.00	.38	.25	.38	.25	.25	.44	1.00	1.25	2.00

FIGURE 2: CHRYSLER. Once more, the chartist paid no attention to the talk about Chrysler, choosing instead to buy when his charting technique indicated he should.

storming to the office to entrust you with their money!"

In a few days, life was back to normal. My work pattern continued as before, my plodding ahead with studying individual stocks and soliciting new accounts. George was, as usual, at his charts every late afternoon. He would not retire as I suggested frequently. Speculation was in his blood. We conversed on occasion about the market, but George seemed stale, with little conviction in his stock ideas. He did some trading, but I gathered from our chats that he was just going through the motions, staying busy, also probing for a new inspiration. I pretty much decided that this usually taciturn, gentle man had had his moment of glory and had returned to mediocrity.

Then, suddenly, a few years later, George literally pounced on me with a maniacal gleam in his eye. It was so uncharacteristic of him. He was almost frothing at the mouth as he exclaimed, "Eddy, I think I found a stock."

I wrinkled my brow and smiled, "Another Standard Gas?"

He ignored my attempt at levity, stared fiercely at my face. "What does C stand for?"

I snarled at the question, "Are you joshing? You know damn well it's Chrysler."

George did not back off. "No. I know nothing about symbols and what they stand for. I just study price formations on charts."

"Don't tell me that you want to buy that piece of junk. They've been losing money or barely breaking even for two or three years in a row. Street talk is that Chrysler is a candidate for bankruptcy."

"But, Eddy, I love the chart. For the first time in a long while, I'm excited about a stock. It's been making a long-term base, and I think it's ready to break out on the upside. Look at this picture."

We huddled over the book on his desk opened to the Chrysler chart, and he excitedly muttered some mumbo-jumbo chart jargon to me. I remind you that at George's encouragement, I had borrowed some of his books about chart theory, had studied them, but I did not pursue the project more thoroughly because it was too time consuming. Still, I was not a complete neophyte.

"Well, friend, it does look interesting. But no thanks. I'm not investing my clients' money in a company that is losing so much money in its current operations. Crazy I'm not!"

"That's okay. But I'm going to buy some tomorrow morning at the opening. And if and when it breaks out over the next few days, I'm going to buy a lot more."

George's speculative thrust took place in the latter part of 1962, and I'm not sure about the number of shares he accumulated over the space of a few days. But I remember watching him pace the office floor, smoking cigarette after cigarette, rushing up to the wire room window, handing orders in to the wire room for submission to the floor of the stock exchange. (That's how it was done in those days.) He half ran over to my desk on the first day of his frantic buying and actually shouted, "Eddy, it's breaking out on the upside above the old resistance. I'm loading up. This is what I have been waiting for!" He behaved more like a mad man than the courtly gentleman with whom we had been associated. Knowing the way George operated, I estimate that he purchased up to 100,000 shares in his margin account over the period of couple of weeks. He was that fearless a speculator.

In the less than two years, Chrysler skyrocketed up almost four hundred percent.

Obviously, the company was not going bankrupt: in the space of a few months, it began enjoying a remarkable earnings turnaround. As George explained it to me one afternoon, "The chart knows everything long before anybody else does."

George had done it again. I never asked him at what price he had sold his stake, if he got out at the top. All he would admit with his modest, disarming smile was that he had made a ton of money in the deal. Using my pencil, I came up with a figure of between one and three million dollars — 1963 or 1964 dollars. I was dying to find out, but it would have been uncouth to question him directly.

Again, I missed another major opportunity. And it was right in front of my nose.

I thought to myself, *Why am I so stupid? Or so timid? Will I ever learn? Will I finally know better the next time? Will there ever be a next time?*

George indeed had his drop dead money now. This time, I decided, he might just step away from the fray. He was getting older. And the slight shaking in his hands was a bit more noticeable.

But he stayed at his desk, seemed so relaxed and mellow, puttering around with his charts during the next several months. He even got out to the club more often to play golf—not too well, by the way. He was so nonchalant when he brought up the subject of cottonseed oil one day.

"Now, Eddy, I know something about this commodity. I've been studying it. I'm a complete dummy about stocks."

"So?"

"Well, I might buy a few contracts of cottonseed oil. Need only a ten percent margin, so the leverage is terrific. I can buy forty or fifty contracts with a relatively small amount of money."

"Doesn't leverage work both ways in case you are wrong?"

"Yes, but you didn't listen to me. I've done all my research. This is a pure supply-demand story. And the chart confirms my opinion."

"Oh, George, why don't you just take your money, run down to Florida, and work on your golf game and drink martinis."

"Not yet. This is going to be fun for a change. Just think, I'll get involved in a deal in which I can use my knowledge."

George was not entering the commodity markets as a complete amateur. He had traded grain on the Chicago Board of Trade: he understood the risks. But his attitude concerning the cottonseed oil was almost cavalier. He had done his background studying, he was in contact with the right experts, and he felt that he had the edge. Therefore, when he bought several contracts of cottonseed oil

11

on the futures market, he was more fascinated than careful. And when the market went against him and broke into new low territory, he violated some of his trading rules: don't fight the tape; when wrong, get out. Amazingly, he bought more. A lot more. Over the years, he had made a practice of buying on short term reactions when the chart was in an uptrend. He would carefully place stop-loss orders in below the market to guarantee that he would be sold out automatically if the price reached a specified low. He had always been adamant against buying when the trend turned down. But here he was breaking all his normal guidelines.

As he rationalized to me, "Don't worry, Eddy. This is different. The market is wrong. Cottonseed oil is bound to go way up again. For a change, I know all of the factors that will bring about a recovery. You'll see."

I walked away from his desk, worried that George might be facing a financial debacle; the leverage in speculating in commodities with only a ten percent margin requirement is so enormous.

I never learned how much money my friend lost in this venture when he finally closed out his position at a huge loss. A half million? A million? More? I don't know. All he said to me was, " I got beat up pretty bad."

I'm sure he had some money left when he retired the next year to live in Florida. I would also guess he continued trading on a small scale. The market was his love.

Then, I heard that his health deteriorated, and this kind of genius of a man died a few years later.

I can recall our last meeting just before he left town.

We shook hands. I thanked him for everything I had learned from our association. In a friendly manner, I said to him, "I always will wonder how you let the cottonseed oil deal compound into a big loss. You preached so much about cutting your losses when you were wrong."

He turned to me and in a mournful voice replied, "Eddy, we're all human."

"Even the charts, George?"

He thought for a minute, then answered, "No, not the charts. The charts are not human."

Then he turned and walked away. I never saw him again.

Dow 1000

A long time ago, I received a telephone call from a friend and teaching colleague at the University of Buffalo.

"Buy a copy of the *Saturday Evening Post* and read the story about Merrill Lynch," he said. "I think you should get a job with that company."

In no great hurry, I eventually did get around to buying the magazine and then reading about "The Thundering Herd of Wall Street." My reaction was immediate. This was for me. So began my love affair with Merrill Lynch.

The challenge was to secure a job offer, no simple matter for a Teaching Fellow steeped in academia and unsophisticated in Wall Street culture. I had doubts about giving up the relative security of a teaching career in favor of pursuing a far-fetched fantasy world consisting of a private office, a private secretary, wealthy clients seeking my advice, big income, lengthy vacations to exotic parts of the world. Nonetheless, I plowed ahead with a series of personal calls on the resident managing partner of the Buffalo office, an E. Howard H. Roth.

Roth's reaction to my overtures was polite, but negative. He was blunt in explaining his theory about teachers not being good candidates for brokerage or money management positions. On six separate occasions over several months, I jockeyed with him, but his attitude changed little. I tried different approaches to win his favor. When I sneaked in that I was Phi Beta Kappa, his retort was a sarcastic, "I won't hold that against you."

As a matter of courtesy, the "old man," as we called him (he was over fifty), allowed me to take the aptitude tests that were customary for job applicants. It developed that I outfoxed myself in answering puzzling questions. For example, naturally, I would rather swim ashore with a knife between my teeth while scouting an enemy beachhead before an invasion than stand back on the deck of an assault vessel with binoculars trained on the target area. My test scores on the psychological testing section presented me as religious, pedantic, idealistic—hardly my true makeup. Roth was satisfied with his negative appraisal of my suitability.

I did score one success when I came up with a clever response to one of his questions.

"What's the stock market going to do, Mr. Polokoff? From your background, you must have some good ideas."

At that moment, I remembered something I had read somewhere, and I responded with a smile. "The market will either go up or go down. In the absence of either of those movements, prices will remain the same."

He beamed. "You are a pretty bright young man. I've been in the business for over thirty years, and I never met anyone who knew what the hell the market was ever going to do."

I was finally making some progress.

In the sixth interview (and by the way, he liked my persistence), Mr. Roth was still feeling me out and had not dismissed my application completely,

"Well, Mr. Polokoff, if I decided to take a chance on you, how much money would you want to make in five years?"

My salary at the university was $3,600 per year. After a moment, I replied, "$25,000."

The manager's eyes lit up. The meeting ended on an upbeat note. Two days later, I was offered a menial job at the local office.

Years later, I learned that the boss had misinterpreted my response to his question. He thought that I had meant $25,000 per year, not for the full five years. Had he realized my sights were so low, he never would have hired me.

I always wondered if he ever changed his mind about teachers. Probably not. As I got to know EHHR later on, I learned that he almost never changed his mind about anything.

Working for Merrill Lynch was quite a step-down from my status at the university. My tasks included answering quote calls, getting coffee for the senior men, keeping charts on price movements for about a hundred stocks and commodities, and servicing the clients of the boss's son. I was pretty much the low man on the totem pole, but I had my foot on the ladder. I had hoped that Mr. Roth would send me to the training school in New York City, but he did not want to spend the money on a questionable risk. Me.

While working and learning, I was also studying for the New York Stock Exchange exam each night. I took the exam without coaching, passed the test, and was promptly allowed to go off on my own to try to build a clientele. Howard Roth's stern instructions to me were almost threatening: "I want you to make personal calls, cold calls if necessary, every day and every night. I want a written report on your call program. I don't want you hanging around the office except for a couple of hours each day."

That was fine with me. I was on my own. It was a challenge.

The Dow Jones Industrial Averages were around 170. Volume on the New York Stock Exchange was running under one million shares a day. The securities business was sick.

At this point, I gave a lot thought to developing a strategy to get going. I was new in the city with few contacts. I had an old Hudson car, a new Indiana wife, but most important, a burning desire to succeed. Buffalo was not a fun city for cold calling, especially in deep winter with swirling snow and gusting winds. But I knew I would work hard from seven to seven or later every day, plus Saturday mornings in the office for planning. But what would differentiate me from others in the business? Why should prospects decide to do business with me? Somehow, I had to sell myself.

I adopted a brash sales approach.

To anyone who would listen to me, and in the beginning, most prospective clients would not even see me, I dwelt on my background in economics at the university, but I also used a little shock treatment in my pitch. "The Dow is going to 1000."

Most people raised their eyebrows as if I were crazy. But at least they paid attention. I was kidded incessantly about my prediction about the Dow. It was a conversation piece. More significantly, I separated myself from the other sales hustlers. I also became skillful at picking winners in the market.

Of course, I was right about my Dow call. The trouble was that it took twenty years to get there.

It was nip and tuck in those early years about staying with or leaving Merrill. The cold calling projects were hugely successful as I brought in scores of new accounts, mostly from the ranks of small businessmen with whom I had developed a great rapport. These hardy rough and tough meat packers, wholesalers in fruits and produce, owners of a large local restaurant chain were risk takers. They knew how to win and lose; they appreciated my work habits, my knack for ferreting out attractive situations in the market, and my honesty.

Living with and working for EHHR was another matter. He was not likeable—at least in the beginning. But he ran the office with skill, and as tough as he was, he was also fair.

I weighed carefully three separate career change offers from three different clients who saw promise in my potential to run a cemetery vault manufacturer, to co-manage a large wholesale food distributorship, to help set up and manage a competing brokerage branch in Buffalo. I stayed the course and focused on Roth's positive attributes.

In the early 60s he introduced a shock wave into my mind.

"Eddy, I've recommended both you and Bill Schreyer for the Merrill Lynch Management Training program. New York is always looking for leaders to run our firm at the higher levels. Years ago, I turned down the same opportunity because I didn't want to get involved in the politics, in the rat race in New York City. Now if you want to move up the ladder, you'll have to accept the challenge."

"What do you think, boss?"

"Well, you're doing very well here. Your future seems assured. Getting in management to take a grab at the brass ring is a long shot with so much competition. I told Bill the same thing, but he'll probably go. He's itching to go, to make a run for the top spot someday. You are more of a market man."

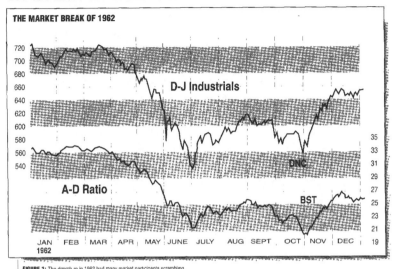

THE MARKET BREAK OF 1962

FIGURE 1: The downturn in 1962 had many market participants scrambling.

I wrestled with the decision for two weeks. I decided that I liked my lifestyle in Buffalo too much and declined the offer. Bill said "yes" right away. He did okay, too. About twenty-five years later, he became Chairman of the Board. When he retired, he donated thirty-million to his alma mater, Penn State.

I never regretted my decision.

I loved the market and the unending battle to outperform. In time, I set up a rough formula for helping clients make money consistently in the market. I studied chart formations for a number of securities, I read research reports from Merrill and other houses, and I read technical analysis reports from brainy people such as Bob Farrell. Mostly, I used common sense and vowed to remain as unemotional and detached from the daily market propaganda as possible. My rules were simple: buy out-of-favor quality stocks with good base formations, avoid popular favorites with big spike-ups, sell into extreme strength, buy when everything seems hopeless, never follow the mob, don't expect to be right all the time, strive for a good batting average, when wrong, take your lumps and get out. I spent an enormous amount of time just thinking. I was blessed with market savvy, something a lot of brokers can't learn.

Came 1962, and my clients were thriving. The general market had been doing well, and even though I have always thought that it is a market of stocks and not a stock market, I became bearish on the general outlook. I recommended a sell program to my customers, but only two heeded my advice to lighten up or sell out. The ensuing break was fierce and relentless—a thirty percent decline in three or four months, even worse for individual stocks. My good call went for naught. Most of my accounts lost on paper a lot of the profits that we had built up so carefully. My client base was in tatters; my psyche was shattered. The market no longer seemed to be so much fun.

One of the two clients who had sold out invited me to stop over to his stately residence on the way home from work to celebrate our good fortune. He toasted my call as we sipped on J & B scotch. "Congratulations, Mr. Polokoff." He was always formal—this wealthy and erudite man of letters. "Your clients must love you."

I replied glumly, "Only you and one other account got out. The rest of my people sat on their hands."

He exploded with rage, "You ought to be ashamed of yourself. You mean to say you do business with people who do not take your advice? You are the professional, and most people know so little about stocks. You are bright. You have a great market sense. Your clients should be happy to have someone like you to look after them."

The client then added, "If I were you, I would never do business with anyone who did not do exactly as you suggest."

That night, I vowed to do exactly what my friend had recommended. Never again would I do business with customers who did not follow my advice.

I had turned a negative market experience into a positive career change.

Then, there was the matter of the Merrill Lynch stock.

To this day, I was never sure if I were invited to join the exclusive ranks of a Merrill Lynch partnership prior to the company going public in 1971 because of EHHR's bulldozing power or because of my success as a top retail producer nationally. I know that he shamed me to buy the Merrill stock offered me by a retiring partner.

"Howard, there must be something wrong with the stock if he wants to sell it. I've got a wife and three kids to support."

Remember, I did come from Poughkeepsie, New York.

Papa Bear turned crimson, stared with contempt as he curled his upper lip—a peculiar facial expression when he became angry, burst out with a rare show of profanity. "Don't be such a fucken fool, Eddy. Find the goddamn money and buy the stock!"

I did.

Once you become addicted to the market, there is nothing quite like the excitement in finding stocks that become profitable investments. Whether you use charts, value analysis, inside information (Shh, that's illegal), ideas of others, hunches, whatever, you just enjoy the thrill of winning and are even stimulated when ventures go awry. Too often we exult in our prescience when it would be more appropriate if we kissed the Blarney Stone.

I was enjoying lunch with a close friend and good client at my city club one day in 1970 when, of course, the market came up.

"Eddy, give me a name, a good stock. I feel like gambling."

"Well, I'm thinking about Syntex. One of our top analysts is high on this drug company because of the birth control pill they have come up with. Women are still hesitating about using it because of potential side effects. But Syntex is a good shot."

20

At the next table was a doctor who overheard part of our conversation. "Excuse me for eavesdropping, Eddy. But I heard you mention Syntex. I'll tell you something about that company that is top secret, that only a few doctors know about. Syntex will soon announce that they have a birth control pill for men."

My face lit up. "Wow. Wait till my golfing buddies hear about this. They'll be jumping. I'm sure they will be giving me a lot of orders the next few days to speculate on Syntex."

A week or so later, Syntex headed for the stratosphere. A few points one day, several points the next week, an almost straight up move from 14 to 59 (adjusted for stock splits) in a year. There was never any information about a pill for men.

My closest friend and best client was one of the lucky ones to ride the Syntex rocket. He advertised far and wide his bonanza and my great call; he was eager to bolster the reputation of Ed Polokoff as a canny stock picker and excellent money manager. In short order, I acquired more new accounts than I could handle. I never peddled stocks again. My career took on a new dimension. I was a money manager.

There is nothing wrong with being lucky. Syntex never did develop a birth control pill for men, but the company made a barrel of money on the pills for women. Years later, Roche acquired the firm.

I was also lucky with the Merrill Lynch stock that I was afraid to buy when it was first offered to me and which Mr. Roth shamed me into buying years ago. I sold my original stock, which cost me sixteen thousand dollars, for thirty thousand dollars three years later in order to buy a house. In retrospect, I should have stayed in that nine hundred seventy square foot bungalow I had been in and sold that first stock for three million dollars forty years later.

I have no regrets. Old EHHR used to preach. "It's better to enjoy your life than it is to make a lot of money." Besides, once the Dow went past 1000, I had it made.

Buy High—Sell Low

Nothing changes.

Everything changes.

For about a half century, I have been complaining that too many research departments, too many money managers, too many stock market "experts" do not perform up to expected standards.

My disillusionment began when I was a young broker in the 1950s. Eager and gullible, anxious to prove my mettle as a bright stock market counselor, carrying none of the baggage of cynicism from experience, I complained to my boss that I was not getting the kind of guidance from our research and other research departments on the street that could help me guide my clients to worthwhile results. Maybe I was frisky enough and naïve enough to think that I could and should always beat the market—especially with good research support.

"Okay, Eddy. Document your case, and I'll set up an appointment for you with our chairman of the board at corporate headquarters in New York City. Present your complaint to him."

Two weeks later, I was sitting in a plush chair across the desk from our CEO in his mahogany-paneled office, detailing my concerns as diplomatically as possible. He was surprised, attentive, sympathetic.

"I'm looking into this matter. We're going to do something about it."

There was no doubt in my mind that he was sincere. It was a happy, exhilarating experience in my early business life.

Since then, I have concluded that nothing much has changed with respect to professional guidance. Only the players and the prices are different. There have been many examples of superb analysts and money managers doing a good job. But in my view as a veteran observer, the percentage of good versus bad is disappointingly low. The "experts" are still prone to follow the herd in suggesting commitments into highly inflated securities and are just as likely to give up on their favorites too long after protracted declines. And too often, when the stocks finally fall so low that there is little risk in instituting positions at depressed prices, the analysts are sitting on their hands. These gurus belong to what I call the "Buy High, Sell Low School of Economics."

Do you remember the negativism on IBM in 1993, the pronouncements that Big Blue was through, and that it was a dinosaur in the modern world? I'll remind you that IBM advanced some six or seven hundred percent over the next seven year period.

Can you recall many research specialists pounding the table, shouting, "Sell, sell, sell," as the technology darlings shot into the stratosphere during the late nineties? The words, which still echo in my mind, are their smug assurances, "These are core holdings for investment portfolios."

Well, core holdings like Cisco went from 5 in 1995 to 80 in 2000 and back to 15, like Corning from 10 in 1998 to 110 in 2000 and back to 5; EMC from 5 in 1996 to 105 in 2000 and back to 5; Intel 5 to 75 to 15, etc. My guess is that the public was left high and dry at exorbitant prices, was gored very badly in their core holdings, was encouraged to get in high, left limping with big losses at lows with the timid sell suggestions coming after the damage had been done.

Is there need to mention the dot-com disasters? Everybody — even non-market people — knows about them. Hundreds of the stocks in this industry went from 50 cents to 200 and back to zilch. A survivor such as Yahoo advanced from 2 in 1997 to 240 in 2000 and now trades around 15. Well, at least it is still in business! I'd be too embarrassed to document the track record of the analysts for this industry.

The poor do-it-yourself IRAers and 401Kers are hunkered down in their accounts, waiting for the magic words to materialize: "the market always comes back." The favorite expression of the neophytes—the Johnny-come-latelies—in the market is, "I can wait. I don't care. I'm in it for the long term."

No comment.

What's a poor investor to do without proper guidance? Buy mutual funds? Maybe. I am, however, familiar with too many examples of poor performance over the years in this area. Perhaps the balanced funds were safest way to go. I venture that those who employed the strategy of buying the S & P 500 and accepted the boring results of doing no better or no worse than the general market averages came out, on balance, the best. Most people, of course, would prefer to beat the market, a normal goal, and certainly a worthwhile project. There ARE some competent guides out there who employ reliable strategies, which lead to superior results.

For instance, I'm sold on the wisdom of portfolio managers who diversify and spread the risk. I saw firsthand the folly of concentrating all assets in one or two stocks. Early on, long before I began managing money for affluent clients, when I was still a stock jockey, trading securities for speculators, I prospected and developed a substantial account of a retired businessman who loved the market. He called the shots; I was but a grateful order taker. He uncovered a great idea in Brunswick, the leader in bowling alleys and equipment. He bought thousands of shares, and he pyramided his holdings with purchases on margin. After a time, I was on record that I urged him to reduce his position, take his profits, which became huge, and run. No way. His ego and self-assurance and greed overwhelmed his judgment. When the boom in the shares ended, he froze and could not accept the reality that the game was over. The decline was precipitous, and because of the leverage of a margin account, he lost several hundred thousand dollars on his lone holding. Not only did he become demoralized, but also he turned to alcohol instead of the market, ended up sick and unhappy.

24

In my opinion, the buy-'em and forget-'em school is not a sure-fire winning approach. It is true that following this edict has created substantial fortunes, but it is to your advantage to understand that such bonanzas often occur because original owners or ground-floor investors instituted positions at very low prices. If an investor or speculator is lucky or intelligent enough to be in early, if he enjoys the ride up and then starts to fret about his large position, then he should sell enough of his stake so that he can sleep well. Once he has that drop-dead money, he wants to be sure that he doesn't lose it.

We are all subject to ignoring an important part of the investment conundrum: there is the buy side AND the sell side. The selling part is certainly as important as the buying part. Selling creates the need to reemploy the proceeds from the sale — an equally important investment decision. When the investor switches, he must be right twice unless he just allows the proceeds to remain in cash for a while. Remember this warning: "reinvest in haste, repent at leisure."

It takes a bear market to remind us all of the fury of a relentless decline. So many hapless market participants are tallying their portfolios these days and moaning, "What happened? How could I go through one of the great bull markets in history and end up with so little to show for my involvement? The markets are up between three and four hundred percent during the last ten years — depending on which index is used. What happened to those projections which promised a ten percent average annual return?"

To my mind, the answer is simple. Too many new investors went to the "Buy High, Sell Low School of Economics."

Eureka

"Wanna make some money, kid?"

"Sure."

"Want your customers to make a lot of money?"

I smiled impishly. "You kidding me? . . . Look, if I can make a lot of money for my customers, the word would spread around. I'll have it made."

"Okay, kid. I'm going to give you your chance. I'll let you know in a few days."

It was a tantalizing encounter. It happened so many years ago that I am surprised that the experience remains fresh in my mind.

The brokerage office at 7:30 on that morning was as quiet as a funeral parlor. The only people present in the boardroom were this stranger, he reading a financial journal, and I, studying some stock research reports.

I had noticed him sitting in the front section of the office reserved for clients for three straight days. I wondered if he were scouting my work habits, especially my being the first one to show up each day. Appraising my work ethic? Before I could satisfy my curiosity by opening up a conversation, he just sauntered out of the boardroom to the exit hall.

I was puzzled. What's with this guy? He looked to be in his early fifties, chunky around the middle, muscular shoulders, dark complexion, bulbous nose, a half smile more sneering than friendly, a full head of wavy, black hair. Italian, Slovak, Jew, Greek? I didn't know or care other than that I was intrigued by the come-on. I was hungry for stock ideas, for clients, for business.

Four days later, I found him sitting right next to my desk, a lone figure in the boardroom. All business, I spoke tartly. I was a rookie broker, but I wanted to act savvy for a twenty-five-year-old.

"So tell me. How am I going to make some money?"

He leaned toward me and answered softly, "Listen, kid. Whatever we talk about is confidential. Not a word to anyone about this conversation. Agreed?"

"Well, we'll see."

"Oh, no. You want to make some money? Mum is the word. Otherwise, we'll forget the whole matter."

He came off sinister, which made me uneasy. Maybe, it was the hoarseness in his voice, the monotone, the steely, penetrating eyes. He acted like he knew exactly what he was doing at all times. *What can I lose?* I decided.

"All right. Mum's the word."

"This is the deal. There's an over-the-counter stock—you can find its price in the pink sheets—called Eureka Oil and Gas. Sells around 30 cents a share. It's going to go to $5 . Buy some for yourself, load your customers up with as many shares as you can buy."

I squinted querulously.

"Let me check the pink sheets."

I scurried to the counter in the back of the office, grabbed the thick stack of pink pages stapled together in booklet form, and brought it back to my desk.

"Let's see. Eureka Oil and Gas," I muttered as I thumbed through the pink sheets. There must have been over one thousand names listed—every stock imaginable not listed on any of the major stock exchanges.

"Oh, here it is. Looks like five or six brokerage houses follow it. Sells for about thirty-one to thirty-three cents."

"That's right," he answered smugly.

"So, what about Eureka? Where can I get some dope on the company? I'd like to know what I'm buying if I buy it."

"Look, you don't have to know anything about this stock. No, that's not right. All you have to know is that it's going to go to five

27

dollars. It's a cheap stock and you can buy thousands of shares. But don't wait. You better act fast. It'll be too late in a couple of months."

I was suspicious, nervous as an expectant father pacing a hospital corridor.

"You pulling my leg? I might be young, but I'm not stupid. How do you know that Eureka is going to five dollars?"

"You'll see. Don't think. Just buy it."

"I'll sleep on it and let you know tomorrow."

His expression turned menacing. "Remember. Mum's the word. I wouldn't want you to get hurt!"

He stood up, shook my hand with a vice-like grip, and then strode out.

I tossed from side to side, trying to sleep that evening, very troubled, very tempted, very scared.

He was again parked beside my desk the next morning.

"I can't do it. Too many question marks. Thanks anyway."

His eyes showed contempt. "Too bad. I gave you the chance of a lifetime. Just remember to keep your mouth shut. You don't want anything to happen to your wife and kiddies."

I shivered as he walked out. *There goes the devil,* I thought. Whatever kind of scheme he was involved in, I wanted no part of it. And I knew I wasn't going to talk to anyone about what had happened.

A week passed by. I continued my routine of prospecting for new clients. Each morning, out of curiosity, I checked the price of Eureka in the pink sheets. It started to creep up. I wondered if I had blown an opportunity. Well, I rationalized: my firm would never have allowed me to solicit buy orders in that stock unless our research department approved the idea. On the other hand, I could have bought Eureka for my own account with my money or I could have gambled on letting some special clients buy the stock through other brokers. If the deal worked, I'd get the credit . . . I stuck to my decision to keep away from potential trouble.

28

Shortly thereafter, with Eureka up to one dollar, I attended the annual meeting of a financial group to which I belonged. As was customary, I exchanged stock ideas with a couple of colleagues in the brokerage business. I chatted with a closer friend, Tim.

"Anything good to buy, Tim?"

He grinned. "If you can keep this to yourself, I'm having some luck with a little gamble called Eureka Oil and Gas. I know nothing about it, but it's been going up. But please, don't talk about it. Sells around a buck."

I was stunned. "Don't worry. I won't say a word."

The allure to jump on the Eureka bandwagon was ever present. The stock was advancing. I needed a winner. I was running into stonewalls in my prospecting calls, and my client list was not growing. Typical of my frustration was my experience with a Polish meat packer.

This one afternoon, I fled the boredom of the office to continue my grueling routine of seeking potential clients. In those days, most people had little interest in the stock market; volume of trading was running something over one million shares a day on the New York Stock Exchange. I was determined to interest anyone who would listen as to the benefits of owning the likes of General Motors, Eastman Kodak, Niagara Mohawk. My strategy of making cold calls was tedious and demeaning.

It was a normal dreary day characteristic of Buffalo in the winter—gray sky, slippery, slushy streets. The weather matched my mood—dour. When I parked my old Hudson sedan in front of Joe Petrewski's sausage plant, I harbored low expectations, but I felt comfortable approaching self-made men, small business owners such as Joe. They were street smart, carried no airs of superiority, and were familiar with taking risks to win or lose in business ventures.

Old Joe was almost fatherly when he showed me into his Spartan office with the big desk and two old wooden chairs.

"Now what do you want to sell me?"

29

"Stocks and bonds. I'm a broker with the biggest investment firm in the world, Merrill Lynch." I handed him my card.

Joe laughed. "I'm not interested. I don't know anything about the stock market. I have enough trouble making money in something I understand—my business, the sausage business."

"Let me tell you about a couple of stocks our research department likes."

"Young man, I like your spirit. It's good to see a guy working hard to make a living. But I figure if your research people have such great ideas, they'd buy the stocks for themselves."

"Try us out. Take a chance."

"Naw. I'll stick to my business. Stocks are a mystery to me."

Joe stood up, a burly man whose stomach showed the influence of too many hot dogs and sausages, shook my hand, and patted me on the shoulder as he led me out of the office.

"When you get something really good, stop back and tell me about it."

I scuffled across the icy sidewalk and entered my mud-splattered car, murmuring, "Eureka Oil. Am I missing the boat? Would Joe have gone for it?"

During the next week, about the only excitement in my business life was following the steady advance of Eureka. Who was buying the stock and why? Was there an illegal pool in operation or was there something to the company?

In a time frame of two weeks, the stock had jumped to three dollars in a quiet market. Still no news to explain the advance. When it leaped to over four a week later, I could not contain my curiosity. I phoned Tim.

"I've been watching your Eureka. What's going on?"

"Beats me. I'm just happy I bought a lot of it for me and my clients. Nothing else is working in this market. Hope you jumped on when I told you about it. Some of my close buddies followed me."

"Nope. I didn't. Just too risky for me."

I was feeling sorry for myself when I hung up. A golden opportunity down the drain.

No more than a week later, Eureka jumped to $4.65, and just as suddenly, the price started falling. In a few days, it dropped to two dollars; ten days later, the price was one dollar. Less than a month later, Eureka Oil and Gas was down to three cents.

I couldn't resist; I was dying to know what had happened.

"Tim, why did Eureka collapse?"

He answered glumly. "Wish I knew. We tried to sell the stock when it got close to five dollars. There were practically no bids all the way down. Buyers just disappeared. Looks like I got stuck in a big hoax. We practically gave the stock away just to get out. Wish I had never heard of Eureka Oil and Gas!"

My tale of mystery or intrigue should end here. I had learned some lessons that would be helpful throughout my career. For example, doing nothing is often a decision and a good one. When you smell trouble, keep away, etc. But how could I know that the mysterious stranger in the Eureka episode would appear some ten years later? I had become a successful producer in the Buffalo office, with a big clientele and a comfortable lifestyle. My cold calling days were far behind. When the office receptionist buzzed me to announce that a Nick Zaranakas was in the foyer waiting to see me, I was startled to recognize the face from the past when he entered my office. I finally got to know his name.

"I figure you would be surprised to see me after all these years. Congratulations. I know you have done well." He shook my hand as he sat down. There were a few new wrinkles on his cheeks, a few more pounds around the middle, and some gray hair streaked through the black.

I was cautious, polite,

"It has been a while. You're looking fine. Can I be of service?" I added playfully, "But please, no more Eureka deals."

Nick smiled. "You could have done well in that stock. You just had to know when to sell."

31

"Just like that. Thanks, but no thanks."

"Mr. Polokoff, forget the past and move on. I want to give you some business. I'm about to put two million in the stock market. Would you prepare a list with your recommendations for a conservative portfolio?"

The man from Eureka, with a name this time, Nick Zaranakas, was again to rattle me. A lure was dangled before me once more, but at this stage of my career, I was hardly desperate for new business. Nonetheless, I mused that a two million-dollar order would be the biggest I had ever had. In spite of uneasiness, I responded, "I'll work up a proposal and mail the list to you. Do you have a mailing address?"

"Sure. I'll look forward to your suggestions." He handed me his card which included his post office box number.

The meeting ended promptly, and as he left, I was harboring unsettling thoughts, such as where would this shady guy come into that kind of money? Was Nick potential trouble? I weighed the pros and cons and came to one of my favorite decisions—do nothing. It was a painful choice because I was always hungry for new business.

A week or so passed. Nick was on the phone. "Where's that list you were preparing? You can't be that busy."

Caught unaware, I answered quietly, "I'll mail it today. Remember that we must have the money before we place any orders for a new account." Inexplicably, I had backed away from my plan to avoid dealing with Nick.

"Stop worrying. You'll get your money ahead of time if I place some orders."

With little enthusiasm, I dictated a letter for my assistant to prepare, which included my recommendations for a balanced portfolio of quality stocks. The project took about twenty minutes as if by rote. I decided that nothing would come of this venture and I'd be just as happy. Or would I?

Nick surprised me the following week when he brought in the check for two million, gave me his bank reference and a Rochester,

New York, mailing address, and other pertinent information validating the account.

"Now, Milton (he still didn't remember my first name), when my check clears, you can purchase all the stocks you have suggested for my account as detailed in your letter to me. I like your selections."

I tried to contain myself because I was shuddering with excitement. Indeed, it would become a huge payday, the biggest in my career, and everything was legitimate. I wasn't sure if Nick were an angel or a devil, and I wasn't about to do research on this enigma.

"Thanks for the order. I trust my picks will do well for you."

That was my last encounter with Nick. He never even returned my telephone calls. Just as mysteriously as he had entered my life, he disappeared completely from my life. End of story? Not quite.

About six months later, my eyes diverted to a corner of the front page of the local newspaper where a story described an apparent murder that had taken place on an isolated road near the Erie Barge Canal outside of Lockport, New York. The slain man was slumped on the front seat of a new Cadillac car with a single bullet hole through his temple. The police identified the victim as a Nick Zaranakas, a private investor, from Rochester. There were no clues or motives for the crime. Investigating police theorized that it was likely a mob killing.

II

About Fascinating People

EHHR

When EHHR finally consented to die at ninety-one, there were few mourners at the church service. Except for Natalie, his fourth wife, originally his executive secretary and quite possibly long-time girlfriend and lover (no one knew for sure because they were both discreet), who dabbed her eyes with a Chanel silk handkerchief. Also the Chairman of the Board, Bill Schreyer, his protégé, had flown in by private jet from New York City to pay his respects. The few wasp cronies he had accumulated over a lifetime were already gone.

Ted, the only heir—the other son had been disinherited forty years earlier—sat stoically in disbelief that the "old man" did not reach ninety-five as EHHR had promised. He had always bragged that he would live longer than his father. I decided that Ted could finally feel relieved that no new humiliations could ever be stacked on him again. Ted never quite measured up in the father's eyes. For years the people in the office talked about the many venomous outbursts by the boss directed at the son at sales meetings on such minor matters as, "How can you be so stupid? A three-year-old child can run that slide projector better than you can."

While the minister droned his brief eulogy, I speculated to myself if the old tycoon had made arrangements beforehand to secure an English country garden setting in Heaven or at least a comfortable spot in Hell—wherever *he* agreed to end up.

His death three days earlier was a shocker—so abrupt. They were sitting at the breakfast table a few minutes before they were to start their journey in his Benz (he bought a new one every year) for the annual spring trip to their second home nestled in a pine forest in Pinehurst, North Carolina. Howard, of course, would have been the driver, colorfully attired in race-car gear, blue beret and all, while Natalie was prepared to supply descriptive commentary during the ride. She adored this patrician gentleman. I remember her murmuring, "God just walked by," when he strolled through the office many years earlier after one of his traditional three month voyages around the world on the S.S. *France* (a way of life, he explained).

That's when I first assumed she was sleeping with the charming reprobate.

While Mr. Roth was Old World elegant, he was also a bigot, a snob, a tyrant, and a mean father. Still, I liked him in spite of the warts. He did own a huge stake in world-famous Merrill Lynch; he ran the local operation with skill and an iron fist. Is that why I overlooked his occasional nastiness? Or was I grateful that he favored me as one of his anointed few, that I had passed muster early in my career, that he had guided me toward wealth and a good life?

No doubt, "Papa Bear," an affectionate term we sometimes used for Howard, enjoyed being my mentor. He was in his fifties, handsome with normal features, always impeccably dressed in a pin-striped suit with conservative tie or wild bow tie, medium height, carrying ten extra pounds on his erect form from gourmet food and extra dry martinis. I was young with little sophistication, energetic, good brains, dedicated to achievement. He was born rich, lived like royalty, and became richer because he was smart. I was lower middle income, accustomed to hard work. I studied his perfect manners and etiquette. At least, I had graduated from Duke with Phi Beta Kappa. EHHR, on the other hand, quit Yale to enlist in the Air Corps during World War I and never got his degree which he didn't need.

The first day in the office, he scolded me as I scurried around, "Take that pencil out of your ear. You're not a clerk. You're an executive."

That's how it went for years. He was tough on me, but I didn't mind because he was fair and I was learning. I recoiled, however, with fury, almost hatred, as his prejudices began pouring out.

Howard referred to Rita, my brilliant assistant, as "a good Nigger" because "she must have white blood in her." He had "no use for most Niggers," he'd say. My colleague, Nick, was a Wop with no Mafia attachments—so therefore acceptable. He became a later favorite. Most Jews were "kikes," but I was fine, "and some of his best friends were Jewish"—an expression that made me seethe. I bit my tongue. He hurled out vitriolic criticisms about Polaks, Chinks, Limeys, etc., as if they were from a different planet. I later rationalized that blue-blood wasps tended to look down on all who were different, on all who had no *Mayflower* roots.

For the first ten years or so of my working for Papa Bear, our relationship was all business, very cordial, Mr. Roth, Mr. Polokoff, etc., until he gave me permission to call him Howard. That's when we established a regular Monday routine of lunch at his establishment club or at my city club where I figured he enjoyed seeing how the rest of the world lived. We always had a glass of port, we toasted L'Chaim, which he tried to pronounce with the guttural accent, and we discussed world events, business, sports, a little sex (no vulgarities, though), everything imaginable. I mostly listened, soaked it all in because he was worldly while I was from Poughkeepsie, New York.

Of course, we talked—or mostly, he talked—about the market and individual stocks. He divulged, using a sweeping oratorical style, tidbits of information regarding companies in which he seemed to have a pipeline to the strategies of the chairmen of different boards. When he referred to a Tom, chairman of this company, or a Bob, chairman of that company, I felt as if I were sitting in on management meetings. Howard pontificated, and I often wondered if it was mostly bluster. Nonetheless, he was the teacher, and I was the student, and of greater importance, he was an excellent stock picker. I aspired to acquire such skill, to emulate his track record although relying in general, on my own techniques. I was not too proud to latch on to Howard's favorites—but with mixed results. The problem was that he would never tell me when he got in or when he was getting out. I can recall, for example, the time years and years ago when I accumulated El Paso Natural Gas, one of EHHR's pets, for several clients at around 20. Six months later, it was down to 10.

"What happened to El Paso, Howard?"

"I got out a long time ago. Broke even. Things change."

I wondered if he gave me the whole story, whether he won or lost in the El Paso venture. You see, with all his connections and brainpower, he could still be wrong. But his ego prevented him from admitting that he might lose once in a while.

Then, there was the matter of the Merrill Lynch stock.

To this day, I was never sure if I were invited to join the exclusive ranks of a Merrill Lynch partnership prior to the company going public in 1971 because of EHHR's bulldozing power or because of my success as a top retail producer nationally. I know that he bludgeoned me to buy the Merrill stock offered me by a retiring partner.

"Howard, there must be something wrong with the stock if he wants to sell it. I've got a wife and three small kids to support."

Papa Bear turned crimson, stared with contempt as he curled his upper lip—a peculiar facial expression when he became angry, burst out with a rare show of profanity: "Don't be such a fucken fool, Eddy. This is a terrific opportunity. Find the goddamn money and buy the stock!"

I did.

Over the years, many of EHHR's pronouncements were hilarious, such as, "Every man should be married three times. In your case, two is just right."

Others were wise: "It's just as important to spend money and enjoy your life as it is to make money."

I was enraptured by his yarns about the "best hotel in the world," the palatial Hotel de Paris in Monte Carlo, with its luxurious appointments, although he later scratched it from his list because the tourists overran Monaco. He even sold his apartment on the Côte d'Azure after seven years of winter residence. Again, too many tourists. He rhapsodized about the four-star restaurant, L'Ousteau de Baumaniere, nestled in the valley below the ancient perched village of Les Beaux near Avignon, France. His mouth watered as he described the bouillabaisse at Tetu at the seaside near Antibes. His eyes gleamed as he talked about touring on the Grand Corniche way up high overlooking the Mediterranean near Nice — although he added quickly that a bigger thrill for him was driving his Alpha Romeo in the trial runs at the annual Watkins Glen Grand Prix near Ithaca, New York, each year.

Almost every Monday, when in town, even long after he had retired, Howard enchanted me with his travel stories to all parts of the world, his often strange, but fascinating philosophies, which I sometimes accepted. I challenged some of his goofier ideas, such as all Democrats were worthless, but he ignored my rebuttals as if they did not exist. I didn't care. I loved to listen and enjoy and often, learn.

When he took me to the Buffalo Bills football game for the first time (he was a lifetime season ticket holder), I was surprised that we sat with the fans in the blizzardly cold and not in one of the glass enclosed luxury suites. It wasn't the cost. Mr. Roth could have bought out the whole stadium, but he wanted the true atmosphere of the game. Of course, he was bundled with a comfy parka and a fur-lined hat. I nearly froze to death. He continued to go to every home game on Sundays until he was eighty-seven.

Some of his quirks? When he entered our house, he walked directly to a painting and straightened its position on the wall. The Kittinger coffee table would be moved two inches so that it would be perfectly centered in front of the sofa. He was such a fanatic on orderliness.

E. Howard H. Roth left this Earth quietly, and he left a lot of money behind for several charities, including my favorite, the Buffalo Philharmonic. There was plenty for Natalie and Ted, too. I'm sure he had arranged to take some with him, just in case.

I've decided he skipped the idea of living to ninety-five because he was eager to find out if there was something else out there on the other side. He had lived his life exactly as he had wanted, and there was nothing more to enjoy.

I fooled him. I took everything he bestowed upon me, but I sorted out the bad and kept the good. Well, not quite. I sold my original Merrill Lynch stock, which cost me sixteen-thousand dollars way back then for thirty-thousand dollars three years later in order to buy a house. In retrospect, I could have stayed in that nine hundred seventy square foot bungalow and sold that first stock for three million dollars forty years later.

I have no regrets. All I was doing was enjoying my success, as Howard had always preached.

Howard was a giant in my life. I gave him nothing. I tried but he would not listen. He thought he was always right on everything. I did not mourn at EHHR's funeral. His death was an exuberant celebration of life.

W.A.S.

The first time Bill Schreyer said he wanted to run the company, I smiled.

He was all of twenty-three with a pudgy, round face, high forehead, smiling eyes, pug nose, a sturdy 5-foot-11 inch frame carrying an extra ten or fifteen pounds. There was nothing in his appearance or personality to suggest a Charlie Merrill, company founder, in the making.

To the contrary, E. Howard H. Roth, resident partner in the Buffalo office, sized him up during their first meeting with: "By the time I get through with you, that wise-guy grin will be gone from the side of your mouth."

Looking back, I realize that Bill's father, manager of the Williamsport office, had requested that his son work under the tough Mr. Roth because Bill needed a little training in arrogance modification, the kind of training an enlisted Marine gets at boot training at Camp LeJeune, Quantico Marine Base. Roth, the martinet, insisted on respect, order, conformity. When he gave that icy stare while barking out an edict, such as, "The only way to do business is the right way" or "When I tell you to work on that underwriting, you better do it," the sales people shuddered. Bill toed the mark, but he managed to retain some degree of independence with his infectious chuckle, his uncanny way of making a clever quip apropos to the subject, his use of a favorite Schreyer expression, "Let's not sweat the small stuff." Roth never taught Bill humility, but he tamed his tendency toward conceit.

Even Win Smith, Chairman of the Board, raised his eyebrows when he interviewed the brash young executive trainee at corporate headquarters in New York City.

"What are your goals at Merrill Lynch, Mr. Schreyer?"

"I want your job, Mr. Smith," came the reply.

Smith later admitted that he had trouble deciding whether he should throw Bill out of the office or take him seriously. "I took him seriously. I guess I liked his spunk."

Very few took Bill seriously—especially in those early days. Nice guy, slightly cocky, was his trademark. On the surface, not an intellectual heavyweight, but bright enough, Bill was a master of focusing his attention and praise on others while downplaying his skills. It was typical of Bill to introduce me to his friends and clients when we were in attendance at a civic function or charity ball or a Jack Kemp fund-raiser with this hyperbole: "The biggest producer at Merrill Lynch and maybe in the country. He does so much business that he gives me an inferiority complex. Maybe I should get into management so I won't have to chase his production figures the rest of my life!"

Always the charmer, Bill had the right word or funny line to enliven a speech. At a United Jewish Fund dinner celebrating the conclusion of a successful campaign, Bill, the only non-Jew in the auditorium and the chairman of the division that raised a record amount of money from the non-Jewish community, was called up to the stage to receive a beautiful painting by an Israeli artist in appreciation for his efforts. Holding up the piece of art and viewing it so that the huge audience could get a glimpse, Bill showed genuine gratitude as he said, "Thank you so much. I'll always remember this wonderful experience. . . . What a fantastic Bar Mitzvah gift."

The roar of laughter and applause lasted about five minutes.

Bill was a good salesman and a successful broker, but not especially astute as a stock picker. One of his biggest clients and a most enthusiastic booster once confided to me that Bill had sold him the worst stock he had ever purchased, Northspan Uranium.

"I know Bill is not an analyst. Who in the world sold him

on that idea! But I still love him and wouldn't dream of doing business with another broker!"

When we were both asked if we had any interest in getting into the Merrill Lynch management program, I quickly declined with no desire to get into the corporate "rat race." My dreams about the future involved hard work leading to a life of comfort—plenty of golf, tennis, world travel, and leadership in community affairs. Bill was quickly enthusiastic to make the change. His fantasy world focused on limos, corporate perks, hobnobbing with corporate giants and world leaders. It was significant that his closest friends in Buffalo were the president of a large local bank, the president of a huge department store, the powerful Mr. Roth (one of the wealthiest partners in the firm), and a couple of well-heeled wasps in the community. No one could fault his selection of friends. It was good business. It was also an early indicator of ambition and wisdom.

"But, Bill. You've got it made in Buffalo. Before long, with your talent and connections, you'll become wealthy. You'll enjoy the good life. You'll run the local operation. ("Papa Bear" Roth was already grooming him to take over as manager when Roth retired.) You'll be the king of Buffalo."

"Eddy, I want to run the company. (*There he goes again,* I was thinking.) I can never do that unless I go through the necessary channels."

"You know the odds are heavily against you. Why gamble?"

"I know, but I'll never be happy unless I try."

What book became his Bible in his How to Get to the Top dream? He did not need the book. He could write the primer!

Bill is one of those rare individuals who mixes in comfortably with all types of people. Put him in a room with fifteen people for thirty minutes, and in a relatively short time, each of the fifteen would feel singled out by Bill as a special person. It's a knack either studiously developed or naturally acquired. His confidential tone and attentive listening as if you were the most important person in the world create the feeling of closeness.

Fun-loving?

There's that old photo of Bill, one of the boys, posing with four other young brokers in front of the fireplace, all extending cocktails in toast fashion, all wearing broad grins, all wearing scissored neckties dangling from their shirt collars. Mr. Roth, local manager, had presented us with these old-fashioned, expensive, but ugly (we thought) ties at an office meeting that day—an office tradition whenever the boss returned from a European vacation. The party that night at my home mocked the award celebration with the tie snipping!

How can I ever forget the afternoon in the office all those years ago when Bill turned to me a desk away and whispered, "Let's go to see *Caine Mutiny* in the theater across the street. There's absolutely nothing going on in the market today. The old man will think we are out making personal calls."

We went and enjoyed the movie.

The move up the corporate ladder was steady. Office manager in Trenton, office manager in Buffalo, district director in the New York Metropolitan area, positions he handled with skill. He broke up the audience of brokers, almost all either Jewish or Irish Catholic, at the first sales meeting he conducted in the New York City district with this comment: "How in the hell is a German Catholic going to run this division?"

That is an example of Bill's incredible way of ingratiating himself with people. But behind that easygoing, friendly demeanor was a bull dog determination to achieve and move up. Every so often I would see him in a new post after a promotion, and he would throw his arm around my shoulder, grin, and say, "I'm getting up there. My goal doesn't seem so far away now."

It was funny, but none of his friends and colleagues in the Merrill hierarchy ever felt jealous or threatened. Actually, a strong group of supporters became like corporate cheerleaders, applauding his progress. He had a propensity to gather around him intelligent, loyal people who enjoyed watching his progress, overlooking his tendency to be too ambitious. It was then that I began realizing that he had a genuine shot at the top job.

When he was promoted to the important position of running the government securities division, after it had stumbled, he greeted his subordinates at the meeting of introduction with a typical Bill approach, "I don't know the first damn thing about government bonds. I'm stupid as hell about this division. You people will have to help me so I won't fall on my face."

Naturally, everybody worked fiercely for their new leader. Bill just knew how to motivate, to lead. He and his gang turned the operation around completely, and quietly, W.A.S. had become a leader with a bright future at Merrill Lynch.

A new face of Bill Schreyer began emerging as his progress toward the top accelerated. There was still the ready smile. There was still the genuine affection for others. Now, more steel showed in his spine. Tough love became part of his arsenal of leadership traits.

Bill demoted, not publicly, but privately and diplomatically, those who did not measure up or messed up, including one of his closest friends. His corps of followers—the FOB'S (friends of Bill)—nevertheless remained strong, committed to his style and agenda as the usual political infighting permeated corporate ranks. There were the so called White Hats, the good guys with humane instincts—Bill's gang—versus the so called Black Hats, the other faction, characterized by callous disregard for personal feelings, the no nonsense, take no prisoners, get the job done crew, the technocrats. The posturing of these rival groups preparatory to the changing of the guard from the Don Regan, Roger Birk regimes lasted several years.

Bill was finally elected to the CEO position in 1985. There were many in the White Hat group who literally cried with joy, and there was a general sigh of relief throughout the firm because of the outcome of the election.

Schreyer wasted little time consolidating his position. He

informed the leader of the rival faction that there would be no upward mobility in his career from that point. He also arranged for his former rival to accept a top position in another industry out of New York City. The FOB'S had prevailed with authority. There have been times when W.A.S. was not exactly Mr. Nice Guy.

Characteristic of Bill Schreyer was his boyhood enthusiasm on the occasion of his triumph. I visited him briefly at corporate headquarters shortly thereafter. He was as ebullient as a Little Leaguer hitting a home run to win the big game. It was refreshing to me to observe this number one man in the biggest investment firm in the world showing me his new office.

"Look, Ed, I have my private washroom, my private exercise room, this fantastic view of the Hudson River and the New York City Bay area, and the Statue of Liberty. Look at this elegant furniture, the mahogany walls, the Kittinger pieces."

"Bill, you really made it. It's marvelous. I'm so happy for you."

"Yeah, I guess I did. Isn't that something!"

One of the striking aspects of his eight-year rule at the top was his knack of breezing through stressful events without losing a step. For example, three months after assuming the chairmanship, Schreyer was dismayed to learn that he required by-pass heart surgery because of some blocked arteries. Quickly and confidently, he underwent the necessary operation, and his recovery was complete.

Then, there was the 350 million-dollar loss suffered by Merrill Lynch when some sophisticated derivative trades went sour. Since this disaster occurred on Bill's watch, there were rumors of tremors in the front office. W.A.S. calmly phoned each director and board member to explain the fiasco: "We had a little problem, which cost the firm over 300 million dollars. I've taken steps to insure that this kind of thing won't happen again. Everything is okay now."

His deft touch with people was masterful again.

Always in the background, never hogging headlines, Schreyer

moved skillfully among the mightiest leaders on the domestic and world scene, continuing the tradition of building up his subordinates and down-playing his role in decision making. It was interesting that for the first time in Merrill history, four or five Jewish executives were sprinkled through the top layer of Merrill Lynch management. Bill played down this coincidence by stating, "I never pay attention to things like that. I'm just looking for the most capable men to run the firm."

David Komansky, current big boss, is the first Jewish executive to run the firm.

When Bill Schreyer retired in 1993, he left behind an aura of good feeling throughout the organization. His reign was significant because tremendous corporate growth occurred during his years in command as Merrill Lynch maintained its position as the leading financial services company in the world.

The Schreyer touch is still intact as he currently serves in leadership roles on prestigious corporate and non-corporate boards, continuing to supply guidance and money to his alma mater, Penn State, including a 30 million-dollar gift to the school. He never misses a beat as the ultimate people person—his greatest talent. He never forgets his roots, Williamsport, Pennsylvania. He continues to call Buffalo, his adopted home, the "best kept secret in America," despite its long decline during the last few years. This Bill has remained faithful to his only wife, the former Joan Legg of Buffalo, has retained his same executive secretary, Ruth Rempe, all of these years, has kept his myriad of friends, has regarded Merrill Lynch as his first and greatest love.

In typical Schreyer style, while providing me with career highlights, he also added this comment: "Eddy, you can write anything you want about me, but of course, you know that I don't like criticism." Then came the chuckle, and everything seemed fine.

My quizzical eye always greets those who question his innate ability. I've heard, "He doesn't seem that brilliant, that special. He's a nice guy, but so what?"

An old friend of mine from Buffalo who knew Bill in the formative years once engaged me in conversation about Schreyer's accomplishments.

" Does he have any money?"

"Oh, I'll bet a hundred or two hundred million."

"Did he earn it?"

"Oh yes, he started from scratch."

"How much money did he make last year?"

"Oh, I'd guess three or four million dollars."

Then came a long pause and finally a dry comment: "He must be a pretty smart guy."

The Odyssey of Alan Chiara

My wife, Gina, had just returned from her class at the museum school, unloaded the art supplies stacked in her arms on the kitchen table, turned to me and blurted out, "I think my teacher is a genius."

"Don't you think that is a pretty strong statement? You're just a beginning student. How would you know?"

She did not flinch and stared at me as if in a trance. "I just know."

It was then that I decided to study this Alan Chiara.

The Los Olas Art Festival in Fort Lauderdale in 1987 was a big event. Lots of people, lots of artists whose works must be juried in before being put on display. A potpourri of food, artifacts, trinkets, jewelry, pottery, sculpture, oils, acrylics, watercolors, you name it—all in an almost carnival atmosphere. I was there doing my research.

As inobtrusively as possible, I watched from a distance this quiet man sitting in a folding lawn chair in front of his tent booth. He looked to be in his early fifties, medium height, athletic build, curly burnt-brown hair, smooth olive skin, a slight bend in his Roman nose, nervous eyes. A rather handsome devil, I thought. What surprised me was that he seemed detached from the busy scene. He was showing, but seemed uninterested in telling about his art—as if it were below his dignity to be peddling his beautiful pieces in such a tawdry fashion. No sales pitches from this proud man!

I finally approached him, extending my hand. "How do you do, Alan. I'm Gina's husband. She's been telling me about your talent."

His handshake was disappointingly limp.

"Oh, she's quite a girl. Good student. Glad to meet you."

Alan remained seated. I ambled around the area, mixing in with several other people who were also viewing the paintings in front of and inside the tent. I mused, *No wonder he wins so many awards at these outdoor shows. Nothing around here comes close to the brilliance of his work.*

That was my first impression. I wandered back to his chair. It was so hot that day—maybe ninety-two degrees—and he was sweltering.

"I'm curious, Alan. How long does it take you to assemble and present this display?"

Emotionless, he responded. "We—my wife, Cris, and I—got up this morning at five o'clock, loaded the stuff in the van, drove over here, set everything up, were ready for the ten o'clock opening. We've practiced so often over the years that we got it down to a science. And, oh yeah, we pray that it doesn't rain."

"How much are you getting for your paintings?"

"Between five hundred dollars and a thousand dollars apiece—depending on a lot of things."

"That sounds cheap to me," I ventured.

"Well, my name isn't Tony Bennett or some other celebrity. But once I win the gold medal at the AWS show in New York City, my prices will go way up where they belong."

"I hear you're a golfer at Boca Del Mar."

"Yeah."

"What's your handicap?"

"Eight."

Geez, I was thinking. *Getting this guy to talk is a major accomplishment.*

"How would you like to be my guest for a round at Boca Grove next Saturday?"

For the first time, he smiled. "I'll be there. What time?"

When I later relayed to Gina my conversation with Alan, she

nodded knowingly. "That's Alan. He's so shy. At class, he hates to talk or lecture. But give him a brush, and he's off into another world showing and demonstrating how to do it. Zip. Zip. Zip. Then you see the most beautiful painting unfold before your eyes. He makes it look so simple. His students are all in awe."

That Saturday on the golf course, he shot an eighty-one because he couldn't putt the strange greens; beat me easily. Over a beer, he opened up.

"My dad, who was a commercial artist, would always prod me. 'Win the gold medal. That's the top watercolor award in America. You're good enough.' "

I learned about his background that day. He was born in Cleveland, studied at the Cleveland Institute of Art and the Cooper School of Art, went to work for the American Greetings Corporation, advanced to the position of master designer quickly. His career blossomed. He found time to freelance; he opened his own gallery, and was soon winning awards at art shows in Ohio. Cris later told me that at age thirty, he won the silver medal at the prestigious American Watercolor Society show in New York City, the youngest winner in history.

"But, Ed, as good as I was doing, I was not happy. I was bored creating florals on cards for American Greetings. I wanted to live where the weather was warm. I wanted to play golf year-round so that I could become a scratch golfer. (The smile lit his face again.) So I gave it all up, and here I am living in Boca Raton, starting all over again with my wife and kids."

Chiara taught watercolor classes at the Boca Raton Museum of Art from 1979 to1991. His students idolized him. They were like his "groupies," exchanging stories among themselves about his idiosyncrasies, his expressions. "Don't be afraid of the paper. It won't bite." Or "Stop being so rigid with your strokes" or "How many times do I have to tell you how to do it," but in a good natured tone. He finally learned how to relax in his classes, even began to teach more verbally rather than instructing by waving about his brush.

I once asked his wife, "How does he get it all done? The classes, the freelance work, the commissions, the golf, the family responsibilities."

"Well, he doesn't sleep much. All his life, he worked late into the night, even when he was practicing to perfect his techniques. He never wore a watch. He would work until the job was done."

His reputation as a fine artist began spreading throughout the Boca community just as it had occurred in Cleveland years earlier. His small home served as his studio for his freelance work, but he needed more space in order to do larger canvasses. Once his income from teaching at the museum and selling at art shows increased enough, he fulfilled his dream of having his own business in the Boca area by taking the expensive but necessary gamble of opening up his own gallery. He devoted extraordinary effort to insure the success of his venture, even giving up his golf membership for a year. Cris organized and ran the Chiara Fine Arts Studio at South Rogers Circle; Gina organized and ran the art school for aspiring painters at the new address. His works sold well at outdoor shows (he won Best in Show awards in Boca and at Los Olas, among other honors) and at gallery openings; his winter and spring classes, four per week, were sold out easily. The gamble had paid off.

Cris laughed as she described an early setback.

"He was the most unmechanical man I have ever known. He couldn't fix anything around the house or studio. I remember when he fell off a ladder replacing a light bulb. He damaged his writing hand (he was a southpaw) so severely that he could not use it for eight months. Alan then began painting with his other hand. He said matter of factly, "You paint with your head and mind, not your hands."

Gina marveled at his Southwestern landscapes and abstracts with their rich colors, Indian and horse scenes.

"It was as if he had lived in New Mexico and Arizona in

another life. The fact is that he had never even visited that part of the country."

Cris chimed in, "Often, I saw him literally throw paint on the canvas. 'What in the world are you doing, Alan?' I asked him.

"Watch," he replied.

"In a few moments, the most gorgeous landscape would start to emerge from his strokes. I'm sure he had no idea what would evolve when he started. It was all from his imagination."

Fellow artist, Bill Griffith, who leased space at a studio adjacent to Chiara and who is a fine portrait painter, once said, "Alan can paint anything in every medium in any style. He is just so incredibly talented and versatile."

Aaron Brand, another colleague and artist, spoke of Chiara's unselfishness. "He was always willing to help, to make suggestions when asked for ideas. He was a wonderful human being."

In February 1994, I revisited my role as observer at the winter show at the Chiara Art Gallery in Boca Raton. The setting was in sharp contrast to the one at Los Olas years earlier when I first met Alan Chiara. A huge spotlight was mounted outside the studio entrance, shooting a bright beacon of light skyward. Throngs of people wandered in and out of the gallery, more than three hundred over the course of the evening. Lavish hors d'oeuvres adorned a large table, covered by an Irish linen tablecloth, set up in the second room toward the rear of the studio. Alan's attractive daughter, Connie, manned the bar just off the entrance, featuring premium brand wines and liquor. Beautiful paintings in a variety of colors, shapes, subject matter, and styles decorated the walls. The Chiara mastery was on full display.

Alan was ebullient, so friendly and uncharacteristically talkative, actually gregarious as he made the rounds among his friends, admirers, and possible buyers. This was not the brooding, reticent artist of years back. He noticed me standing aside viewing the whole scene, and he hastened over to my side.

"Ed, everything is going great. We've sold a lot of paintings tonight. And would you believe that I'll be working on fifteen new commissions over the next couple of weeks."

"Well, it's about time you got hot. I never doubted that this day would come. Congratulations."

At that point, his smile faded, his face turned serious.

"I'm still remembering my dad's words. 'Go for the gold.' Well, I think I have a good shot at it this year even though the competition is so tough. You know, about two thousand paintings from the top artists in the country are being judged by a distinguished jury of top water colorists for the American Watercolor show in New York City this spring. I submitted 'Hidden Canyon.' It's an abstract with great design and stunning colors. The kind of thing that is popular with judges these days. The painting shows a lone Indian astride a horse surveying the haunting landscape. You might not like it as much as some of my florals and mountain scenes—the pretty things. But, Ed, an art critic might label it a masterpiece."

"Good luck. If you win, you'll probably get so cocky you won't give me the time of day."

"Naw, I'll just have more time to become a scratch golfer and beat you for bigger stakes."

At the end of the evening, Gina walked up to Alan and said, "We bought too much wine. There's a lot left over."

Alan grinned, "Put it in the refrigerator. We'll have a party when I win the gold. I don't think a Boca resident ever won it before."

Everybody—Cris, Gina, especially Alan, a couple of his special friends—was tired, but on a high after a long, exciting evening. Alan was as happy as I had ever seen him.

Saturday night at a Valentine's Day dinner dance at Boca Del Mar Country Club, Alan and Cris were still in a celebration mood, enjoying a last dance after a fun-filled evening. Suddenly, Alan stopped, gazed at Chris and mumbled, "I feel a little dizzy, honey."

In a second, he collapsed to the floor and died instantly of a heart attack. He was fifty-seven.

Four days later, his wife, mother, five children, close friends had gathered together at the Chiara home after the funeral service at the St. Joan of Arc Catholic Church and the cemetery burial. Eyes were red, tears were still flowing, and hysterical sobbing intermittently broke out.

The telephone rang.

"Please answer it, Gina," Cris begged Gina. She was still crying uncontrollably.

"I will."

"Hello."

On the other end of the telephone, "Can I please speak to Alan Chiara?"

Gina was fighting back her tears. "He's not here."

"Well, I have some good news for him. Last week, the judges of the American Watercolor Society Show had voted his work, 'Hidden Canyon,' the top painting in the exhibition. He has won the gold medal. We want to congratulate him."

Gina could barely talk. She was numb.

"Thank you. I shall tell his wife and family. Alan died Saturday night."

"Oh, my God! We are so sorry. We never knew."

Two months later, at the annual awards ceremony for the American Watercolor Society at the Salmagundi Club in New York City, Cris Chiara received the gold medal award for her late husband.

At first, Cris determined to keep the masterpiece for herself in memory of her husband. This year, I convinced her that the painting would best perpetuate his legacy if it were part of the Boca Raton Museum of Art's permanent collection. Therefore, she consented to sell "Hidden Canyon" to my wife, Gina, and me so that we could donate it to the museum. The stunning work is now on display by the entrance hall at the Boca Museum's recently renovated Art School on West Palmetto Park Road where Alan once taught. The official appraised value of the piece is ten thousnd dollars.

I always think of what might have been whenever I look at Chiara's masterpiece.

III

About Turning Points

Just Say No

The cocktail party at our home for major contributors was a fitting prelude to the Danny Kaye Benefit Concert set for the following night at Kleinhans Music Hall. We knew Danny would conduct the orchestra with his usual mixture of talent and humor; we already knew that the Buffalo Philharmonic would benefit from the most successful fund-raiser ever. I was exultant as chairman of the event, but weary when the last guests finally said "good night."

Looking back, I had pushed too hard. Danny had established his usual tough terms: he would perform for free if we guaranteed that every seat in the house was filled. How surprised we had been to learn that it had been no easy task selling out the house at premier prices. Perhaps, Danny Kaye's star power was behind him.

We were asleep after midnight, but about 2:30 A.M., I awakened Gina with the complaint about strange pains in my chest. She quickly called our doctor and friend, Del, who was at our house in fifteen minutes. A careful checkup, some reassuring words, a couple of Valium, and I was asleep comfortably for the rest of the night.

The next morning I was up early, fumbling with the laces to my sneakers, preparing to go to the tennis center for my Saturday game when the telephone rang. Del's tone was friendly, but terse: he would pick me up in a few minutes for a trip to the hospital.

"And bring an overnight bag. We want to check you out to make sure your heart is okay. And don't plan to attend the Danny Kaye concert tonight."

Hospitals are a sobering reminder of our mortality; often you enter and wonder if you'll ever leave. I was subjected to tests, consultations, the angiogram. Then the waiting and worrying, the trying to relax, the trying to doze off, but no luck. My mind was full of unsettling fears. What would the angiogram show? Could I really have a heart problem? Three days ago, life was beautiful, but now —

I opened my eyes as I sensed my wife's entry into the quiet room. The glum look on her face was not a portent of good tidings.

"Any results from my angiogram?" I asked anxiously.

"Well, I just saw the angiologist in the hall. I'm afraid you'll need by-pass surgery. You have a blocked artery."

Those words rattled my nerves. We stared at each other morosely. Then she added as cheerfully as possible. "It will be a routine operation, and he said you'll be back to normal in a few weeks. He also said that without the operation your life can never be normal again."

A flood of fear and anger rushed through my veins. How could this be? My health had seemed great. And now, change.

During the next hour, we began adjusting to the realities confronting me and us, and we even began discussing the possibility of early retirement. The mood was definitely downbeat.

Shortly thereafter, Dr. Del walked in accompanied by a stranger.

"Eddy, I want you to meet Dr. Black, a cardiologist from another hospital. I hope you don't mind that I called him in to review your case. He knows his business, and I have the highest respect for his ability."

"How do you do, Doctor? This is my wife, Gina. So, when is the surgery?"

"No surgery for you. You're going home tomorrow. You have a blocked artery, but it is a secondary artery. I would never suggest an operation on a secondary artery. Your main arteries are clear!"

"But the angiologist said that — "

"Eddy, you are going home tomorrow. You are fine."

"Can I play singles tennis?"

"You can do anything you want. But I want to see you next Wednesday at my office."

Hello, sunshine! Smiles were lighting up the room. In an instant all the gloom had disappeared.

The next day, I did play tennis, and how ironic that on the next court was the angiologist. I nodded to him coldly. I dared not talk to him for fear that my inner rage would burst out.

The conference with Dr. Black on Wednesday was an event that changed my life forever. I sat across the desk from this slight, wiry man with the goatee, the clipped British accent and the confident voice.

"From now on, Eddy, your favorite word is 'NO.' You've been running 150 miles per hour for the past thirty years, and your body is rebelling. You can conduct your business normally or you can stay involved in your community activities, but you no longer can do both. If you do decide to stay in business of managing money for your clients, you must get rid of any account that gives you stress.

"In addition, I am changing your diet and your eating habits. Low cholesterol, low fat. I'll give you the sheet detailing the does and don'ts. I'm increasing your exercise routine. Plenty of walking briskly, more tennis, etc. Finally, you must reduce the stress level in your life. Some stress is okay, but it must be manageable. When we get through with this lifestyle change in your routines, your heart will be stronger than ever. Any questions?"

The meeting lasted no more than fifteen minutes.

I remained active in my business, enjoyed the most productive years of my career, and eliminated most community activities. A friendly "no" became an important word in my vocabulary. And my new lifestyle routine is twenty years old and still counting. Yearly, I visit Dr. Black for an extensive examination, and he claims my heart is stronger now than it was twenty years ago.

The angiologist received an important promotion a couple of years later.

The Embrace

We embraced one last time standing in the open doorway as the sun rushed in to bless our decision.

It was not a sexual expression as our arms squeezed tightly around each other. For those emotional twenty seconds, my soul was whispering,

"No. No. This marriage should be salvaged. There have been too many cherished moments together which bind us. There is still time to turn back."

I did not cry, but I wanted to. I was grieving the death of a marriage. The pain seemed unbearable.

Flashback scenes were racing through my mind.

The mini-picnic on the summit of the highest hill in town. It was a lose-our-virginity adventure—everything discussed and planned beforehand as if copied from the text of a play. The seclusion and quietness of the spot looking down the valley to the city below, the purchase of the expensive condoms advertised to maximize pleasure, the extra handkerchief in case there was a mess, the thin blue blanket to place over the grass where we would lie.

We did the act, performed clumsily and quickly, trudged down the slope to the populated area, wondering,

"Is that all there is? Where were the bells?"

The next time, the sex improved and became satisfying.

I remembered her words of caution when we eloped against the wishes of both families: "We are really different in too many ways."

I was older, all of twenty-one, to her nineteen, and I rejected and smothered all doubts. The marriage of the ambitious Easterner to the gracious, somewhat timid Midwesterner worked well for many years. However, my rapid business and civic achievements propelled me on a fast track, which created a continual stream of stressful encounters for her. At charity balls, she was the most beautiful girl on the dance floor with the warmest smile, but also with a severe migraine headache. She dreaded air travel, but she managed to suffer through. She had no interest in golf or tennis or sports—my hobbies.

But as the mother of our three children, she excelled. It was she who sat around the kitchen table with the kids and their friends late into every night when they were in high school and college, smoking cigarettes, drinking coffee, swapping stories, listening, laughing at jokes, playing scrabble—the eternal deeply-loved den mother. In contrast, my role as supporting actor was minor. I studied, worked on my business, enjoyed the weekly night out with the boys at the club downtown, often turned in early with the warm tones of happy conversation flowing from the kitchen downstairs soothing me to sleep in preparation for the early trip to the office the next day. If I were almost a "scratch" golfer, she was definitely a "scratch" mother.

The years passed quickly, but our drifting in different directions accelerated. The outside world hardly noticed, but we did, as did the kids who were then in college and high school. Her headaches and backaches became more frequent.

The fateful night at Dorado Beach, Puerto Rico, flashed into view. We had been to one of those business cocktail-dinner parties, which she endured and had returned to our beach casita. With the orange full moon beaming a swash of light across the gently undulating waves in front of our beach house, with the graceful palm trees swaying in the light breeze, with the fragrance of gardenias intoxicating the air, we sat on the beach chairs to soak in the lovely setting. A tempting scene for lovemaking, I presumed.

She then spoke slowly, softly,

"I think we should get a divorce. . . . We are on different

paths. . . . I warned you when we first were married. . . . It will get worse in time."

For moments, I froze in disbelief. I shocked myself when I did not protest sharply at once. I remained silent. . . I finally responded, "Whoa. Wait a minute. We've had some problems. Most married couples do. We can work things out. We have too much going for us."

"Well, I've given it a lot of thought. I think it will be better for both of us in the long run."

The friendly, matter-of-fact conversation went on for a half-hour or so, and we decided to delay the breakup for two years. By then, our daughter, the youngest, would be entering college. Also, we would have ample time to reconsider the heavy decision.

I look back and marvel at the civility of the episode. Then, there is another aspect. Was she searching for a way to tell me that in order for our marriage to survive, I would have to readjust my lifestyle to a slower pace to conform to her personality? She was not strong enough to change. But I was. Did she secretly hope that I would firmly squash the proposal? When we retired for the evening, my mind was in turmoil. She had dared uncover a smoldering box of troubles.

The two years flew by, and we agreed that divorce was preferable to growing frustrations. The children were not surprised, and they were mostly supportive, especially the older two. Those last weeks before the separation were full of melancholy.

Then, the final good-bye in the sun-lit doorway.

Remembering the Six-Day War

It was the same feeling—the feeling I had during the war before an invasion. No appetite. Dry mouth. Nervous small talk. A brave front. But way inside, fear.

It was Buffalo. It was June 5, 1967. Yet, it was D-Day all over again.

The same feeling.

Fear.

It was The D-Day for all Jews for all time. Way inside, we were all afraid.

At the office that day, I carried on by rote. Quieter and with more intensity. Almost in a daze.

My mind whirled furiously—a lightning flow of thoughts.

My past, the present, the future. Over and over and over again.

Especially the past. Painful memories kept flooding my brain.

Like the day those two older boys jumped on me while I was walking home from school. I was small and no match for their strength. Finally, some older friends came to my rescue. "Why pick on Eddy? He's a nice kid."

One of the fleeing bullies turned around and shouted back, "He's a Jew, and we don't like Jews. They're all no good. Hitler was right."

I remember the front-page pictures in every daily newspaper of Nazi storm troopers beating Jews.

Each morning, a new photo to sicken my stomach before I went to school.

Even at college, with all the pleasant memories, there were those black moments.

That Southern boy on the baseball team. The first day of practice, he said aloud and mockingly to me and everyone, "Jews are bookworms. Not athletes."

That did it. I won my letter because I had to prove that he was wrong . . . Jews were always trying to prove something in those days.

I remembered Father Coughlin and the German-American Bund and the Nazi concentration camps and all the ugly anti-Semitism very much in the open in the 1940s.

I used to say to myself in those days, *If only there was a homeland for the Jews, a psychological crutch on which to lean, a place for secondary allegiance. Other minorities had that. The Italians have Italy. The Irish have Ireland. But the Jews had no ace in the hole. It was here or nowhere.*

My mind flashed to the present, that day, June 5, 1967.

I was secure, happy, and comfortable in my environment, accepted as a normal American with perhaps a little added status because I was a Jew. Yes, it had become almost "in" to be a Jew.

I thought of my three children. They were baffled by my references to anti-Semitism. They hardly knew it existed. They didn't have to prove anything to anybody.

Then I thought of that tiny haven, that psychological crutch, that Israel that I used to long for. I knew that since that little nation had come into existence, everything had changed for the better.

And now, Israel was in mortal danger. I felt helpless and frustrated.

So I waited. We waited. The world waited. The world was standing by again, watching and waiting just as it did years ago when Hitler was murdering human beings who happened to be born Jewish.

The horrible specter of possible defeat terrified me. Defeat meant barbed wire and prison camps and Arab savagery and mass murder and rekindled hatred and prejudice. A new Hitler—Nasser—would be working at solving the Jewish problem. His method would be a continuation of Hitler's solution—genocide—and then there would be the biggest United Jewish Appeal campaign ever to save whatever was left of the Israelis.

How lonely the Israelis must have felt that day in June. There had been some protest against the Arab menace. But the traditional friends of Israel seemed paralyzed and impotent.

A curiosity seemed to grip the fancy of the world. What were the odds for Israel's survival? How would this collection of refugees, this grab bag of persecuted and harassed oddities from all over the world—this traditionally non-militaristic people—do in battle alone?

The Jews in their customary role—the underdogs. Most civilized people felt sorry for the Israelis.

I was tired of the world feeling sorry for the Jews and doing nothing about it.

So were the Israelis.

They fought.

They fought for survival. For our honor. For our dignity.

Alone.

Not with the UN intervening in 1948 to establish a truce.

Not with the British and French as in 1956—however small their participation.

Alone.

Surrounded . . . against dreadful odds.

We silently implored that these brave people would not perish.

The drama, the courage of that moment of confrontation will be described with awe by historians a thousand years from today.

Winning was not easy. The stories about the fifty-one heroes written up in the *Jerusalem Post* attested to that.

But the victory was quick and decisive.

A miracle—the Israelis call it –"the miracle."

First disbelief, then relief, then pride, overwhelming swelling pride. After centuries and centuries—a winner!!

Never in all history had the Jews carried their heads so high.

We were floating in euphoria.

Some day we shall look back on these incredible events and tremble with emotion. We have seen the establishment of a little state whose accomplishments in a short period of time are so remarkable that they defy description.

It is not the lot of the Jew to have tranquility and happiness so easily. The war is not over. Peace has not been obtained. When the Israelis finally achieve their goal—peace with safety. And they will. When they finally make it. And they will.

Then, all Jews all over the world will have made it once and forever.

Addendum to "Remembering the Six-Day War"

This essay is actually my speech at the major gifts' banquet of the United Jewish Appeal in Buffalo in 1968. I was the youngest chairman of the Fund Drive in Buffalo history.

At the conclusion of the address, there was absolute silence in the room. Then followed a huge outburst of prolonged applause.

The man recognized as the leader of the Jewish community and a major contributor to local charities, stood up, glanced around the room, waited until there was complete quiet, then spoke: "That was the greatest United Jewish Appeal speech I have ever heard in my life. And I've heard a lot of them. I'm increasing my pledge by twenty-five percent over last year's gift."

His generosity became contagious. One by one, each of the two hundred men at the fund-raiser, arose and announced his increased pledge. A record amount of money was raised that evening for the cause.

Bill Schreyer, at that time office manager of the local Merrill Lynch operation, who later became the Chairman and CEO of Merrill Lynch worldwide, was the only non-Jew at the dinner. He was serving as the chairman of the non-Jewish community division. Sitting next to me at the dais, he leaned over and whispered in my ear, "Ed, this will be the highlight of your life."

In retrospect, it was big—but not that big.

Over the years, I have used the tired expression in many of my talks at seminars and lectures: "Seize the moment." I didn't know it then, but that is exactly what I did that night.My life in the public arena changed almost instantly. In time, I became chairman of the Buffalo Philharmonic annual campaign, then Board Chairman of the Orchestra with Michael Tilson Thomas as conductor, followed by Chairman of the Governing Committee of the Buffalo Foundation. In 1977, the *Buffalo Evening News* selected me for the outstanding citizen of Buffalo award.

It seemed that everything started with my Six-Day War speech.

IV

About the Early Years

The DSP

It was the summer of 1940. It would be the last summer of our innocence and idyllic bliss. Dunk, an atheist and a wasp, was going to Albany State; Shea, an agnostic and a Catholic, was scheduled for Notre Dame; Polokoff, a secular Jew, was boning up on the North versus the South before entering Duke. We gave ourselves the title, the "DSP" and vowed to become the third and greatest triumvirate.

The days flowed together as we drifted into a routine: walks up and down Main Street and bull sessions late into the evening. The cross-seeding of contrasting philosophies and opposing viewpoints sparked our brains. D, the philosopher, the teacher, the poet, dominated the conversations because he loved to shock with outlandish statements. S was so unsophisticated in the ways of the world that he devoured every radical morsel of fact and theory as truth. I enjoyed the non-stop dialogue and offered my idealism.

We were blood brothers; we held back no secrets as we explored the mysterious crevices of our souls.

The conversations revolved around sex, girls, religion, virginity, God, masturbation, and other things, such as sex. While every aspect of erotic sexual behavior was debated fiercely, the dominant theme centered on whether or not we should maintain our virginity until marriage. The DSP arrived at a consensus—no sexual intercourse until marriage. This acceptance of abstinence as a way of life presented challenges in our relationships with girls. We remained dedicated to our pledge despite libidinous activities in the back seats of cars, on living-room sofas, and in secluded areas of public parks. We managed to get our release from sexual tensions—and I'll leave that to your imagination—but I cannot vouch for whatever sexual satisfaction the girls could attain. We remained virgins, we were honor-bound, and we were proud of our behavior. Nonetheless, were the truth to wiggle out, our deep-seated strength sprung more from the fear of inflicting pregnancy on our girlfriends than on goodness. A realistic assessment of our conduct would have contradicted our supposedly high moral standards. Our sexual adventures were not lily white.

The summer ended, and we continued our dialogue through the use of a scroll, which passed by mail from South Bend to Albany to Durham and around again until a new scroll had to be started again every few months. The communication became a long running séance. With World War II suddenly upon us, and with D and S in the army reserves and P in the naval reserve, the arrival of the scroll was a respite from the worries about the future. How lyrical Dunk's words, how naïve Shea's words as he labored to break off from the grip of a strict parental upbringing.

One day, the following spring, a letter arrived from Shea`s brother. An eerie foreboding made me fumble as I opened the envelope. S, the good one, the purest of the DSP, the one who was lucky enough to get the safe assignment of serving as a cryptographer at an air base in India, had been killed in a freak accident on an airport runway. My head throbbed. I wandered aimlessly for hours. I cried inside. He was gone forever, and yes, he died a virgin. The DSP could never become the third and greatest triumvirate.

The following summer, I met my wife-to-be, and Dunk became unimportant in the new scheme of things. Moreover, his brooding eyes, his laconic speech, his lascivious stare made my girlfriend squeamish. Dunk and I drifted apart.

As for the DSP vows of chastity until marriage, my virginity was soon gone. My love partner became my wife, and it was not a marriage of necessity.

The DSP died completely after Dunk and I returned to college after the war. He became a Professor of English at a university, later the head of the department, and I learned from a mutual friend that he married one of his students. I also learned from the same friend that during the summer of innocence, Dunk was sexually involved with a seventeen-year-old slim Italian beauty who lived next door to him—and at the same time, with an older blonde bombshell who taught him all the tricks about love-making, which he never passed on to us. To this day, I still wonder why Dunk wasn't completely honest with his blood brothers. I felt betrayed.

All that is left of the summer of innocence are six scrolls laden with the thoughts and dreams of the DSP. On rare occasions I retreat to my study, remove the scrolls from a secret hiding place, and read with amusement and nostalgia about those wonderful days of naïveté. What we did, should have done, could have done are all unimportant. We were growing up, maturing, enjoying friendship, learning about life.

I realize now that it was not a summer of innocence.

Boyhood Memories

"Hey, Dave, you think you have a future president there?"

Dad nodded approvingly as we walked hand in hand past his storefront window at the Farmer's Market. "You never know. He's a nice little boy."

A lot of people would tease him that way. He was so proud of me.

Years later, after I had achieved some success at Merrill Lynch, my mother, in her own way, elevated me to a presidency. We were spending a few days at the then famous Concord Hotel in the "Borsht Belt" of the Catskill Mountains outside New York City for a family reunion. At lunch one day, we commingled with a couple of other families sitting at a huge table, enjoying the typical Jewish pigout of corn beef, hot pastrami, lox, bagels, blintzes, and fifty other goodies conducive to early heart disease. Naturally, the bragging-rites ritual started among the mothers.

"My son is a Hollywood producer. And you ought to see his *shiksa* wife. Like a movie star."

Then, the next mother jumped in. "My son owns a chain of grocery stores in New Jersey."

We had told Mom about my recent promotion to a vice presidency at Merrill, one of several hundred at the firm. Mother was not going to be upstaged.

"Eddy, my son, was just elected president of Merrill Lynch."

I blushed at this preposterous statement. I rebutted briefly and changed the subject. It would have been futile to explain to Mother my exact status. She never did figure out what I did for a living.

If you had known my mom, you would bet that her son would

not be presidential timber. She must have come through Ellis Island in the early nineteen-hundreds, but I'm not sure. No doubt, her mother did. I never learned the true story because Mom told so many different versions of her childhood. Dad, born in Poughkeepsie, said his family roots were in Brest-Litovsk on the Polish-Russian border.

Mother alternately bragged or complained, depending on her mood, about working in the sweatshops in the garment district on the Lower East Side of New York City. A matchmaker arranged a meeting between my dad and this attractive blonde from Brooklyn. It was love at first sight. She was fifteen; he was twenty. He rescued her from atrocious working conditions, brought her to Poughkeepsie, New York, and married her immediately. There had to be some kind of ceremony: hanging on the living room wall in their house was a big photograph, framed in glass, of a gorgeous girl and a sturdily built man in tuxedo, both smiling broadly.

Dad's father, Max, was a strict, by the book, religious zealot who attended shul every day. Mom called him a rabbi, but that was probably an exaggeration, as were many of her statements. Anyhow, Grandpa would have insisted on a formal ceremony, marriage certificate and all.

The "rabbi" was a grouchy, heavily bearded martinet. Mean and demanding, he made all of his kids toe the mark—and there were eleven of them. Sadly, six succumbed to illness in their early years. Sicknesses, which are considered routine now, were often fatal then. Grandpa showed what little affection he had for anyone to only me—for reasons no one ever knew unless it was that I was a cute little guy with yellow blond hair and an ever-present smile on my face.

The day Max took me for a horse and buggy ride in the country still remains in my memory. The buggy was quite a sight as it crawled along at five miles an hour, with its high wheels attached to the sides of the wagon. My family was worried about my safety because horse-and-buggies just did not seem safe on cement highways with Model T Fords whizzing by at thirty to forty miles per hour; it was likely the only old-fashioned vehicle of its kind on a main country thoroughfare in Dutchess County. I remember Mom's voice as we approached Grandpa's house after we had returned from the four-hour country excursion around Pleasant Valley. "They're back. Thank God. Thank God."

Everyone had been so nervous. Including me. But I didn't complain. I just faked having a wonderful time.

When Max was on his deathbed a few years later (I think he was in his fifties, but he looked about one hundred—people in those days died so young), the entire family had gathered at the patriarch's house to pay last respects. I was singled out at his request and was led into the dreary bedroom. He reached out for my hand, drew me toward his lips, and whispered hoarsely, "Promise to put on the *tefilin* every morning and pray."

The religious rite of placing leather type straps around the hands is still observed by Orthodox Jews. I trembled, afraid of God's wrath if I said no. So, I mumbled, "I will."

When I left the room, I rushed to Dad's side to report the conversation. He became angry when I relayed Max's request. "Forget it. That's not for my boy."

I did, but I remained nervous for years about my not keeping my word.

It was strange how quickly Dad gave up interest in formal religion once Max died. It was his way of rebelling against the stifling strictness that he had been enduring all his life. Once Grandpa passed away, Dad attended the synagogue only for Rosh Hashanah, Yom Kippur, or special events such as Bar Mitzvahs, weddings, or funerals.

There was another remembrance about my relationship with Grandpa. His house on Jefferson Avenue was well within city limits. Behind it in the backyard was a small barn for his horse. The barn was quite the conversation piece, being the only one in the city. I loved it. Many a day, I visited the old man, loaded hay in the barn's bin, climbed up the ladder, jumped from the high loft into the hay mound below, repeating the procedure many times. It was great fun for me while Grandpa thought I was being such a good boy for helping to feed his horse.

A favorite memory about my first home was the ice manufacturing plant directly across the street. I spent hours standing on the platform in front of the large open doorway, which exposed the great pool where water was frozen. I watched the automated process of the machine slicing up huge blocks of ice and moving them to the area where trucks sat ready for loading. Ice delivery to homes was a big business, and iceboxes in homes were the refrigerators of the day.

My worst memories were the black eyes and bloody noses I suffered from fighting the anti-Semitic big bullies in our lower income neighborhood. The constant barrage in the press reporting the Hitler propaganda against the Jews never seemed to end. I hated what seemed like inflammatory rhetoric.

My parents owned a two-story clapboard wooden house consisting of four flats. We occupied an upstairs flat—living room, dining room, three bedrooms, kitchen, and two bathrooms. On freezing, wintry evenings, Mother often turned on an electric heater beside her bed for additional warmth. Early one night, while Dave was still at work, my brother and I heard a screaming from her bedroom.

"Help! My nightgown is on fire from the heater. I'm going to burn up."

We rushed into the room, grabbed the blanket from the bed, and smothered out the flames. She was slightly singed.

When Dave arrived home later, he, who almost never swore, exploded in rage. "I knew we should never have bought that goddamn heater. Throw it out of the house."

He had already vowed to move into a better area; he worried

about my fighting the roughnecks. Now he realized that he also needed a house with a more modern heating system. In a few months, we moved to a superior location two miles away.

I was eight years old, and I didn't have to read the Bible to learn about heaven. It was College Hill Public Park, directly across the street from our new residence. The park was vast—four miles in circumference, with gradually rolling slopes leading from all sides to the plateau top. From the summit, there were spectacular views of the Hudson River and the Catskill Mountain foothills for miles around. Spread around the park were tennis courts, space for baseball and football games, hills for skiing and sledding, fields for track sports and almost every game imaginable. Finally, there was a fine public golf course, which I never considered using. Golf was for sissies!

My priorities were sports, sports, sports, and then girls. Never tall, but always muscular, I had hoped to grow higher—especially for basketball. My baseball coach in high school preached to his players, "Don't smoke."

In my case, he was particularly adamant. "Polokoff, don't ever even think of taking up smoking. If you do, you'll never grow. If you want to get to the big leagues, you've got to get bigger."

Well, I never smoked, but I still didn't grow much, and I never got to the big leagues.

Bigotry cursed most of my early life. I warded off the unpleasantness by immersing myself in athletic competition. Bold headlines sensationalizing Hitler's hatred of the Jews, pictures in newspapers and magazines showing European Jews being herded into railway cars like cattle for shipment to concentration camps, served as fuel igniting latent anti-Semitism. I fended off so many prejudicial remarks, such as, "Didn't the Jews kill Jesus?"

"How come the Jews have so much money?"

"Why do the Jews always stick together?"

The blot of subservient behavior during the Hitler days was finally erased years later by Israel's heroic victory in the Six-Day War against the Arabs in 1967. World Jewry released unbridled revelry, a pent-up reaction to centuries of persecution. I remember how proud I was in that period as were all Jews throughout the world.

However, in my youth, my feelings were quite different. I felt ostracized until I cultivated several friendships with Christians. It took years before I escaped the feeling of isolation. Was I ashamed of my heritage? No. Just at a handicap.

Being a member of a minority did not seem to bother Johnny Tanner, a black kid about four years my elder, who lived across the street two doors up. The word, "cool," fit Chinkelstein's lithe and smooth presence. He enjoyed that nickname, but where he got it, I don't know. A familiar sight every night was "Chink" holding court under a streetlight with five or six of us enraptured by his words of wisdom about sports and girls. He was a speed demon in track events, a colorful storyteller, a hero and guru in our eyes.

Chink and I often walked home from school together after classes in the afternoon. On this one day, we were accosted by some older hoodlum types who began taunting us.

"We don't like niggers and we don't like Jews. Hitler is right. We're going to beat the shit out of you."

We tried to ignore them, but they became more abusive. A small crowd gathered as they began to push us around. Then, the fistfight erupted. Badly outnumbered and outfought, we were knocked down. Suddenly, a speeding youngster ran into the circle of combat and confronted the attackers.

"Leave 'em alone. If you want to beat them up, you'll have to lick me first."

Dick Whitesell, a boy about one year older than I, had seen the commotion from a distance, rushed over to help out. I barely knew him other than hearsay that he lived in an all-black neighborhood. He was the top athlete in high school. The bullies went after him, but he turned his fury into a whirlwind of blows until the four of them were bloodied and badly beaten. Chink and I added some support, but it was largely a one-man show of grit and power. Dick was struck many times; he too was bleeding. But he never stopped advancing and pummeling until the bad guys ran away.

"Good thing you came along, Dick. We appreciate what you did."

He threw his arm around my shoulder. "Eddy, if anyone ever bothers you or calls you names again, just let me know. I'm taking care of you from now on. You can call on me too, Johnny, if you need help."

Dick became my friend and protector. He was a legendary type of person, the defender of underdogs and harassed kids in school. In later years, he won a scholarship to Syracuse University where he played baseball, captained the football team, was an All-American candidate, missed playing in the big leagues as pitcher because of injuries sustained while playing football.

The 1930s were Depression years. It was common for beggars to stop by the back door for food and mostly coffee. My parents treated them kindly. Our family was poor, but never in want of food. I can remember how hard my mother, Rose, and my father, Dave, worked as a team. Often, they would be up late into the night, sitting at the kitchen table poring over the records to make certain the budget was in balance.

In the wintertime, the business was raw furs, which involved the collection of skins from trappers and hunters and the reselling of the merchandise to manufacturers of women's coats in New York City. In the late spring, summer, and fall, the business consisted of my dad buying fresh fruits and produce at the New York City or Albany terminals, transporting them to Poughkeepsie via large trucks, and reselling the merchandise to store owners, peddlers, and nearby summer camps. The food business was especially arduous, with Dad sleeping no more than four or five hours each night. His routine of accompanying the driver of a huge truck to and from the market terminals three or four nights a week was fatiguing. Mom, with minimal formal education, learned to help with the bookkeeping. These businesses barely survived the hard times, but were successful enough to provide the family with decent shelter and to put nourishing food on the table every day.

Some of my fondest thoughts were of summer vacations at Camp Boiberick, one of my Dad's customers for provisions each season. It was located twenty miles from Poughkeepsie in a country setting of gently rolling hills surrounded by densely wooded forests stretching toward a higher elevation. An irregularly round lake one mile in diameter with trees, bushes, shrubs lining its shores in a nearby valley was a focal point for camp activities. The complex itself consisted of a large dining hall, twenty cabins near the woods for campers ages six to sixteen, basketball courts, two baseball diamonds, an arts and crafts center, an auditorium, an administration building, ten buildings across the campus for adults, and of course, the swimming and boating area near the lake.

With few exceptions, everyone at the camp was Jewish—the college-age counselors, the help in the dining hall, the administration people, and the campers. They were "Noo Yawkahs" from the grimy, gray Bronx, and most of them had never seen the verdant scenery of a Camp Boiberick. The curricula included water sports, hiking, competitive sports, and learning. Food was good. Everything added up to eight weeks of healthful enjoyment. During my five years at the facility, I attained a type of celebrity, being a kid from the country among all the city folks. I thrived in the environment, excelled in sports, especially baseball and track.

Team rivalries added excitement to the season with the final week featuring games to establish champions in each sport. My greatest asset was speed, and I still have a picture showing me sprinting over the finish line to win the hundred-yard dash.

On the last day of camp, prizes were handed out to the various winners during the final assembly at the auditorium. There was also suspense related to the naming of the Golden Boy—the outstanding camper of the year award. Dave and Rose beamed in the audience as I was called to center stage to receive the honor. Rose nudged Dave. "He's such a good boy."

Dad just smiled.

Years later, I reluctantly concluded, looking back, that Mom was having an affair with the lifeguard at camp. I also recall how she constantly complained about her boring life.

"You never take me anyplace. We never go dancing. We don't go to parties. You're always tired. When you do have a day off, you fall asleep listening to the ball games on the radio."

Dad finally suggested, "Why don't you go to Camp Boiberick for a couple of weeks? The change will do you good."

Dad was glad to get her off his back. He loved his little business, but it required exhausting physical work and long hours with little time for adequate sleep. Sex was no doubt relegated to secondary importance. However, sending Rose to camp was like feeding kindling wood to a smoldering flame. In view of the idyllic pastoral setting, I can rationalize, but not justify, Rose being easy prey to the overtures of the handsome, sandy-haired lifeguard down at the pool near the lake.

I was surprised the day Mom took me for a ride in her car to the nearby village and invited Josh, the lifeguard, to accompany us. I was even more surprised to see her fondle him in the front seat while I sat in the back seat, to see them kiss passionately as they left the car to enter the general store.

"Now, Eddy, don't tell your father. He might get jealous."

I remained mum, and I also never mentioned that Josh and Mom often walked together across the campus into the woods. I never caught them in the act, but I have no doubt that the muscular guard had plenty of energy for my frustrated mother.

There were other incidents that lend credence to my suspicion about her sexual proclivities. For example, there was often noisy commotion in my parents' bedroom next to mine. The heavy breathing, moaning, grunting, crying out alarmed me. One day I asked my older brother, "Were they fighting last night?"

"No. They were just screwing. Your mother gets carried away. She's hot stuff."

I now look at the bright side: I'm grateful I inherited some of her ardor!

To this day, I feel that I never really knew or understood my complex mother. She was attractive, curvaceous, although a bit heavy in the breasts. Her face was happy, flirtatious, and friendly with blue eyes and smooth skin. Men took a second look when she strutted down the street as if she were a Hollywood starlet posing for the camera. However, her obsession with personal appearance as the most important part of life annoyed me—even into later years. It seemed incongruous to me that a woman in her eighties after a hip operation would continue to wear high-heeled shoes in order to show off her still shapely legs. Dad regaled her with affection and treated her like a goddess on a pedestal. Unfortunately, she was unable to shuck off the coarseness that stemmed from her rough and tumble sweatshop days.

As a mother, she deserves high marks. There was always a good meal on the table at regular hours, the house was clean and orderly, there was dependability to her care and presence. We were fed a constant barrage of morality.

"Now, Eddy, don't get any girl pregnant. It's wrong. Besides, she'll make you marry her." It never occurred to Mom that I intended to remain a virgin until marriage.

We were lectured, scolded, occasionally punished with the strap for disobedience, with Dad assigned the job of inflicting three or four belts across the bare buttocks. She was strict, but not oppressive. I was taught responsibility, but given freedom.

In family and social circles, she was not well liked. Not only self-centered, Mother was also overly possessive. For example, Dad had always enjoyed his younger brother's company and had managed to set aside time to fraternize with him. She discouraged this friendship by making disparaging remarks about brother Irv and his wife; Mom didn't want Irv to cut in on her time with her husband. Eventually, Dave and Irv became distant. Another example involved my younger sister and her husband-to-be. Mother became jealous when marriage loomed on the horizon. Mother's reaction was selfish: she would be losing a daughter and a close friend. My sister's priorities seemed unimportant to Rose.

Mother's interest in sex was often humorous. She reminded my wife, Gina, that oysters would be good for my sex life. After Dad had died, Rose was courted by a kind, stately older man who doted on her. She first sought family approval before the relationship developed.

"You don't mind if I go out with Lou? He's always chasing me. But he is Italian."

Gina replied, "Go ahead, Mom. Have a good time. Just make sure you bring the kids up Jewish and not Catholic!"

A couple of years later, I inquired, "How are things going with Lou?"

Mother, in her eighties, replied seriously, "Oh, I think I'm going to drop him. He can't get hard. He's not interested in sex."

All things considered, though, she was a good mother to me.

My parents referred to Bill Clinton, behind his back, as "Goofy Bill"; he was partially retarded and quite dumb. Big, brutishly strong, kind, immensely loyal to my family, Clinton was the all-around handy man around the house. Where Dad discovered him remained a mystery. Bill lived alone a few miles away, and the normal sight was his arriving by bicycle each early morning to work at the house or the store at the Farmer's Market. At the fruit and produce business, his tasks were all physical, such as loading and unloading trucks, lugging heavy crates and sacks of merchandise. In the fur business, his work consisted of scraping skins and mounting them on wooden boards for stretching and drying in the backyard garage in preparation for sale to New York fur coat manufacturers.

During idle periods, Bill sat on a chair next to the stove in the kitchen, like an obedient dog awaiting instructions from his master. Rose was the master, giving orders for him to vacuum, dust, mop the floors, do the dishes—all the chores of a domestic. Small wonder the house was usually so immaculate. Mother exercised magical powers over his mind: he seemed dazzled by her good looks and was quick to carry out any request. I later wondered if a sexual relationship had developed between the two. As simple as he was, Bill was masculine, thirty-ish, smiling, harmless. I mused about the amount of time they were alone together in our house. I never caught them in the act, but nothing would have surprised me about my mother!

At age eleven or twelve, after I had already sensed sexual stirrings in my body, I was traumatized by a personal encounter with "Goofy Bill." By chance one afternoon, I wandered back to the garage, opened the door, confronted the handy man exerting rapid hand manipulations on his unusually large, ramrod straight penis. I stared at the scene, eyes agoggle. It was the biggest penis I had ever seen.

"Bill, let me touch that big thing," I blurted out.

Blushing, ashamed, he turned away as he shouted,

"Get out of here, Eddy, or I'll tell your mother what you said."

I fled the garage, flustered and distressed by my automatic reaction to the scene. Bill and I never discussed the incident. It was the only homosexual inclination I have ever had in my life. In later life, I've wondered to myself if my sexual inclinations would have included homosexuality along with my normal desires had I masturbated Bill that day. Is it possible that an experience such as this could lead to dual sexuality?

When I reminisce about my dad, my thoughts race to baseball and how much he loved everything about the game. Too busy to play or practice excepting on weekends, he played catch with me for a few minutes almost every day. I was the little five- or six-year-old pitcher, serious about trying to throw the baseball to the target, the mitt held stationary by the crouching receiver, my father.

"Come on, Eddy, put that ball right here. Make believe you're pitching for the Dodgers."

We had such a good time pretending to be big leaguers. The bonding of father and son was a beautiful thing to behold.

Dave managed, coached, and financed a local ball team—the Jewish Center Stars—for a couple of years. I was such a little tyke, but an enthusiastic mascot and batboy for the team. Every Sunday, there would be a game with a neighboring rival organization at the ball diamond in a public park. Dad arranged everything: hiring the players, scheduling the games, buying the equipment and uniforms, conducting practice sessions, paying expenses. The games were played in an oval-type stadium, with bleachers lining the first base and third base boundaries: the outfield had no fence, but was surrounded by tall elm trees sporadically growing ten or fifteen feet apart about 360 to 450 feet from home plate. A hard hit line drive into the outfield would often lead to a home run if it got past the outfielders.

The games were played in a lovely pastoral setting, and the fans enjoyed good baseball. My recollection is that a hat was passed through the stands and around the outfield and the funds were distributed to the players on both teams—according to my dad's allocation. Occasionally, a couple of stars were brought in to attract a larger crowd, and they were paid more than the regular players were. I'm sure Dad made no money on the games, but he just loved the action. Those were the Great Depression years, and finally, after a couple of seasons, the Sunday games just ceased. There was not enough money to keep the competition alive.

My dad was so likeable, with a sunny disposition, but he had his quirks and prejudices. For example, he was opposed to Jewish people marrying outside their religion. My younger sister, a pretty girl with blonde hair, a slender figure, nice complexion, was popular with the boys in high school. One high school boyfriend became very attached to her and began talking about marriage. Once their dating became steady and serious, my father forbid her from seeing him again—almost keeping her confined to our home. The suitor's only negative in my dad's eyes was that he was a Christian. In time, they broke up and my sister ended up marrying a fine Jewish boy two years later.

Back in those days, intermarriage was rare. My father was angry with me when I was courting my non-Jewish girlfriend in South Bend while I was at officers' training school at Notre Dame. He warned me that if I ever married her, he would never speak to me again. I refused to be cowered, and we married immediately after I graduated and just before I shipped out to the Pacific. It was an upsetting experience, but with a happy ending. The day before I shipped out from Gulfport, Mississippi, for duty in the South Pacific, I received a telephone call from my dad: "I forgive you, Eddy. I bless your marriage. Now good luck overseas and come home safely."

Of course, I was grateful for the reconciliation. But at that stage of my life, I was more concerned about surviving in a war than violating a Jewish tradition.

Confrontation

The time for procrastinating had ended. The day for action had finally arrived. It was 3:45 on a clear, chilly morning, and I sat on the passenger side of the front seat of the pickup truck in front of my home waiting for my dad to come out of the house. Strange that I would be so serene and nervous at the same time.

For two weeks—no, more like ten years—I had been steeling myself for this day. I had drained my mind of second thoughts and a sense of inevitability had settled in. At last, Dad emerged, and we started the ten-minute drive to his place of business at the Farmers' Market. Usually, we exchanged small talk, but on this ride, there was little conversation. I wondered if he sensed my anxiety. I wondered how he would react to the pending confrontation. No turning back now.

I had enjoyed the work at the wholesale fruit and produce business each morning for the past five summers. It was mostly strenuous, physical labor, such as unloading the big truck laden with crates of oranges, lemons, grapefruit, plums, melons, and sacks of potatoes, onions and other items for sale to the merchants and peddlers who did their buying each morning between 5:00 and 8:00. The merchandise would be neatly stacked in front of Dad's warehouse-type store and in the cavernous interior. Samples of delicious fruit would be strategically spread out so as to be available for tasting. There was something cozy about this market place scene with my father performing as salesman and smiling raconteur and the customers sampling the colorful displays of tempting fruits and produce. I did a little selling myself, but mostly, I, with two other workers, unloaded the big truck, and I also lugged sold packages to areas designated by the buyers. I liked the atmosphere: Dad's sales techniques, the peddlers' corny jokes, the delicious, healthful food, the brisk morning air, the muscle-building labor. And—this particular summer, I was almost like a celebrity.

"Eddy just finished his freshman year at college. He made the Dean's List and he played freshman baseball," my father beamed.

Not many kids went to college in those days, and the fifteen or twenty buyers milling around liked to hear about me. Eddy was going places, they would think. He would end up a doctor or a lawyer or maybe a big league ball player.

In another forty-five minutes, my brother sauntered into the area—late as usual, and my mind turned to the messy business ahead. My mouth tightened, my heartbeat quickened. The morning air suddenly seemed heavy.

My thoughts wandered back to an instance of necessary violence in my life. It was when I was a third grader in the public school, an unhappy time for me because a big kid in my class had been continually pushing me around and taunting me with surly comments about my being a Jew, about Hitler being right. Finally, little me, skinny and timid, stood up and fought back with my hands and body, and in the brief skirmish with my tormentor, I suffered a bloody nose and several painful blows to my stomach. I lost the fight, but the bully never harassed me again.

Then my memory flashed to my last two years at high school and to my hero, Dick Whitesell, and to his inspirational presence in my life. He was the best athlete in the school; he later played varsity football and baseball at Syracuse on an athletic scholarship. For some reason I could never quite understand, he was my self-appointed protector, my bodyguard. True, I was small, but strong, and certainly no sissy. But Dick automatically watched over his friends and all underdogs and harassed weaklings. It was so ironic that Dick lived in about the toughest, most impoverished neighborhood in town, part of the only white family in a black ghetto, and yet, he never cussed, never chased girls, was always the polite gentleman. Everyone knew his father was an alcoholic; we knew nothing about his mother. The famous fictional hero in those days was Frank Merriweather, the All-American Boy. Dick was Frank!

And I knew well that Dick could and would fight with his bare fists. Every so often, he had invited me to be part of his entourage of spectators at a grudge battle on a specified evening date in a secluded part of the City Park near the reservoir on top of the hill. His fisted opponent was always a powerful, older kid, usually a roughneck, a gangster in the making. Dick, the champion, the king of the turf, was constantly challenged by these low-lifes, and he never backed away. It would be a gruesome battle in front of fifty or sixty kids siding with one fighter or the other—but not interfering with the fisticuffs—and the vicious encounter would last fifteen minutes or so. Dick never lost, no matter how bloodied or battered. He would simply stick it out until his rival would quit. I was grateful that he would be at my side if I needed him. This day, however, would be my personal battle. I had seen violence. I was mentally prepared for a fierce, bloody match. I wanted this battle, I needed this battle, I was ready. I, too, would stick it out.

During the past year at college, for my exercise and physical fitness class, I had elected to take boxing for one semester. The course was not exactly fun. The instructor was kind, but clumsy, a former nearly punch-drunk boxer who did not appreciate his own strength. Occasionally, he would punch too hard, not intentionally, and many a day, I would show up at the next class, English, with a bloody nose or a welt under my eye. But I did learn to box and fight and suffer pain. For me, it was a necessary learning experience.

I would shortly test my skill.

How can I explain my brother's erratic behavior, alternately, mean spirited and then charming. A first child, he was adored by his mother no matter how unpleasant and sarcastic he would be to her. My father worked such long hours that he hardly had time to discipline him or control his wildly swinging moods. I was never able to decide whether he was a bad seed or a spoiled kid. I avoided him as much as possible to keep some kind of peace in the family. Somehow, I managed to enjoy a happy childhood with good parents, a loving younger sister, and a strange, older brother.

He was second in command in the business, a good salesman, bright and funny at times, but at other times, unpredictably nasty in speech and temperament. Three years my senior, he was somewhat bigger and heavier, a wise guy with a cigar in his mouth and a foul tongue, and he had opted to skip college in order to make money, buy new cars, bum around with girls of questionable moral standards. I watched him strutting around that morning, making wisecracks, waited for him to approach me with his usual peremptory orders and berating comments. My anger mounted as I recalled how he used to push me around, kick me in the rear, pound me with his fists when I was small and incapable of fighting back. In those days, he had even taken dead aim at my legs and behind with a Beebee gun and had shot pellets at me until my Dad had taken the gun from him. He still had the tendency to push me around, to ridicule me. Well, this day was the day of reckoning.

He approached me with a sneering voice. "Get a move on and get that truck unloaded, you lazy ass!"

I fumed, "To hell with you. Do it yourself!"

"What did you say, you little jerk?" he glowered at me, pushed his nose close to my face, gave me a vicious shove.

My fury erupted. "Don't push me around." I said, "Do it yourself. You're all through bossing me around."

"I'm going to beat the shit out of you," he snarled back.

"Try it. Put up your dukes." In an instant, a ghostly silence settled over the area. Everybody was suddenly watching this drama unfold. Time seemed frozen.

I confronted him in a boxing stance with my fists extended outward toward his face. Angry and surprised, he wound up and threw a powerful right swing at my nose. I blocked the blow with my forearms, countered with a hard smash to his cheekbone, and followed through with several rapid shots to his stomach. Furious, he peppered me with several hits. My newly acquired boxing skill could not ward off all of the blows. Then followed a furious exchange of hits and misses, and blood flowed from each of our faces. Bare fists are wicked instruments! The scuffle lasted less than five minutes. No one, including my dad, interfered in the brutal exchange. I was hurt, but I bore in relentlessly, much the superior in skill and my furious attacking finally knocked him down. He jumped up quickly, surprised, embarrassed, hurting, stalked me a few seconds, and then abruptly turned around and walked away, bloody and bowed. He had quit! He left the scene.

Just as quickly as if nothing had happened, time was unfrozen, and the market scene reverted to the normal morning routine. There were a few smiles on the faces of the merchants and peddlers. I heard a voice in the background shout, "It's about time you took care of that bastard!"

My dad gave me a handkerchief to wipe the blood from my face, patted me on the shoulder, and returned to the business at hand.

V

About Days at Duke

Indoctrination

It was Saturday night, the first weekend of the beginning of a new life for the incoming freshmen at Duke University. The excitement became contagious as the new students wandered from room to room on the second floor of the dormitory to make introductions and small talk. Somehow, a group of ten or twelve ended up at Tom Kingston's room, next door to mine, because Tom, by nature of his outgoing personality, became a focal point of interest. He was on a football scholarship, he was handsome, he shook hands and patted backs, he smiled all the time, he told short jokes with elan. No doubt, Tom would become a BMOC (big man on campus).

By ten o'clock, a genuine bull session was in full progress with the lively conversation jumping from Yankees, Rebels, religion, sports, girls, and you name it. The dinky room was packed with a few of the guys sitting on the two beds, several sitting on chairs dragged in from adjoining rooms, five or six standing around. I enjoyed the scene, drank it all in, marveled at the varying dialects: the drawl of the big black-haired guy from Mississippi, the BAAS-TON accent of Byron, the slang from the NEW YAWKER, the Y'ALLs from the Carolina contingent, the Midwest twang from the Chicago kid. The ribaldry increased as acquaintances achieved familiarity. Fun and camaraderie became co-partners.

I loved it, my first taste of college life. I had never been away from home before; the 1,500-mile distance from Poughkeepsie meant freedom and independence. I just kept grinning. I was no longer just Ed; I was Polo or Apollo, nicknames Tom gave me with affection. I was already one of the guys.

Tom suddenly stood up from his slouched position on the bed, held his hands high above his head, and raised his voice above the din.

"I know the location of a good whorehouse over in Raleigh. A couple of my buddies have been there. Let's drive over tonight and celebrate. The girls are supposed to be beautiful and (chuckle) . . . talented."

A few "yeahs" greeted the proposals initially, and some enthusiasm slowly spread to most of the others. I demurred meekly at first with the excuses such as: "It's been a long day and I'm tired. Raleigh is too far away."

"Only thirty minutes," came the rebuttal.

"I'm afraid of syphilis."

"I'll give you a rubber if you want," Tom came back.

The adventurous segment of the group was persuasive. I was not about to throw cold water on a hot project. Once I signed on, all but one or two became enthusiastic, and soon, our newly acquired friends who had cars were enlisting passengers. I decided not to admit that I was still a virgin because I did not want to lose face with my new friends. Deep down I was terrified by the thought of VD, but I was also prepared to unshackle some of my boyhood inhibitions. I'd go along and see what happened.

Our procession of four cars stopped at a tavern outside of town for a couple of bracing beers, and our spirits were high. We then proceeded to the little house on the outskirts of Raleigh. Tom knew just where it was. A friendly woman greeted us at the door; I figured she ran the business. We politely walked into the living room.

By now, my heart was pounding, but I became more relaxed as I surveyed the comfortable, but bizarre setting. The living room consisted of three worn sofas, two stuffed, upright sitting chairs, a couple of end tables, two floor lamps—everything surrounding a plain wooden floor set up as a dancing arena. A record player sat on a table in the far corner, and strains of "Stardust" wafted through the air. Several attractive young girls attired in bright-colored, but inexpensive evening gowns engaged the newcomers immediately, and before long everybody was dancing or chatting amiably. *Man*, I was thinking. *This is great. I love to dance and nuzzle with a pretty partner.* It seemed all so proper and romantic.

In a few moments, the dance floor had emptied, the pairings evolved naturally as the guys expressed their preferences for mates. I noticed that the honey-voiced brunette with the trim figure and I were the only ones left on the floor. My partner squeezed my hand and led me toward the staircase. I became nervous because dancing seemed preferable to my displaying my inexperience and ineptitude in whatever lay ahead.

"I've saved a special room for us upstairs. You are going to have a wonderful time," she cooed.

I followed sheepishly, and whatever sexual desire I had accumulated disappeared in a second as we entered a plain room with a bed and a chair and an overhead ceiling light. She remained coquettish and also businesslike as she sat on the bed next to me.

"Would you like to leave the lights on so that you can see me or would you rather do it in the dark?" she asked. She was starting to disrobe while I remained frozen.

I answered quickly, "Let's turn them off."

By now, she was naked, and she started to caress me.

"Aren't you going to take your clothes off?"

I was embarrassed; I felt foolish. A silence permeated the darkness.

"You're scared . . . Are you still cherry?"

"Yeah. And I just don't think I can do it. I can't even get it up. I'm really sorry, but I'll pay you. But please, don't tell the guys that I chickened out."

"Look, I can't take your money unless I give you some kind of thrill. I'll jerk you off. You'll like it."

In about ten seconds, she worked her magic on my previously dormant penis. It was over so quickly that we both laughed loudly. I was happy to pay for her services.

I walked downstairs and waited for the rest of the gang to congregate and exchange stories. Everybody seemed so giddy and boastful. I displayed my full quota of braggadocia. Tom hastened over to my side, threw his arms around my shoulders, and blurted out, "Now, Polo, aren't you glad you came along?"

"Damn right. Best piece I ever had in my life!"

My buddies never did find out what had happened to me on that night. It was my indoctrination. I had become one of the boys.

First Impressions

How cruel of the editors of the Duke University humor magazine to display the ludicrous portrait of Stan on the front cover for student amusement and ridicule. It was not as if he were like the *Time* magazine MAN OF THE YEAR. Rather, this uncaptioned picture made my freshman roommate look more like the campus FOOL OF THE YEAR. You see, Stan, while not ugly, was certainly funny looking. His curly, shooting-up-in-all-directions, black hair stood too high on his head, his thick horned-rimmed glasses hid tiny deep-set eyes, his nose was pushed in almost like that of a prize fighter, his lips were thin and unsmiling. His complexion was dark because even after a shave, his black whiskers were too dense.

We who knew him regarded him as a beautiful, brilliant, warm human being. As the magazine circulated around the Duke campus, I wondered how Stan could remain so stoic while others were snickering about his grotesque visage.

I admit that when I met him for the first time, my reaction was unhappy. By chance, we had been matched to spend our freshman year together as roommates. On that first day of college, when I entered the small spartanly furnished room, there sitting at the desk reading a book was this man who looked old enough to be my father rather than a college kid. *Could this be my roommate?* I wondered. Apparently, yes.

After awkward greetings, we tried to make friendly conversation, but he seemed so gloomy for a seventeen-year-old with the dry, emotionless voice. I panicked, decided that I had to change as quickly as possible for a different roommate. My first impression was that we were acres apart in intellectual interests, social inclinations, and athletic prowess. He was a loner, I was gregarious. He was a pedant, I was a jock. He liked to read books, I liked to fantasize about girls. He was Albert Einstein, I was Jack Armstrong, the All-American Boy. A combination of him and me would never work.

I was ashamed of my negative attitude. I remembered the slogan, "Never judge a book by its cover," but for some sophomoric reason, I was doing just that. Our dialogue during those first few weeks was limited and formal, mostly because I remained standoffish. He, on the other hand, showed a genuine interest in my aspirations toward making the freshman baseball team and in my forays over to the Women's Campus seeking excitement with girls. Grudgingly, I began realizing that he was an okay guy—different, boring, by my freshman standards, but okay.

And yes, he bordered on genius. His curricula consisted of the tough pre-med courses, but he did his homework in a flash. When I was stumped with math or chemistry, he helped quickly. In a relatively short time, a procession of students from our dormitory came by almost every night for assistance, and Stan never said "No." He was the fountain of knowledge, and among his student colleagues, he was their savior before exams. Often, at 1:00 or 2:00 A.M. while I was trying to sleep, he was still patiently tutoring any or all who needed help. Laconic, odd-looking, dull, but an angel.

I was well along in my decision to move after the first semester. One evening, two months into the term, we were quietly studying our respective assignments when I ventured, "Stan, I intend to move in with Jimmy next term. You know him. He is my close friend from high school days, and we always wanted to room together."

He looked up slightly and replied in a matter of fact manner, "I understand. I don't blame you. He's a nice guy."

And in a couple of seconds, he added, "Do you want to go over to Art's room in the next building? He has some cold cuts and crackers for a little snack. We can talk and listen to some music."

"Sure. Thanks. That sounds good."

I had known Art slightly, but he was Stan's close friend. He was a foreign language major, the son of a college prof in a New England school, a charming dilettante, a lover of classical music, a shy, smiling kid.

We entered his room to the strains of a beautiful symphonic piece playing on his record machine.

"What's that?" I asked sheepishly. I loved music, I played jazz piano, but I was used to Count Basie and Duke Ellington.

"Tchaikovsky's *Pathetique*. One of my favorites," Art beamed.

"How absolutely beautiful," I murmured. I had never heard it before. In fact, I had listened to very little classical music in my life.

That evening proved to be a real treat for me. Art and Stan conversed animatedly about opera, baseball, the voluptuous blonde in the zoology lab, life after death, famous composers. I joined in hesitantly because I sensed my inadequacies in the company of two very intelligent individuals.

Over the next two weeks, I joined Stan and Art for the midnight goodies a couple of times, even though I felt intimidated in this atmosphere of condensed brilliance. As it turned out later, Art finished first in his class among all freshmen, Stan finished second. Without my even knowing what was happening, I started to aspire to emulating their scholastic performance, even though I still preferred my baseball and petting escapades. No doubt, their brainpower was starting to rub off on me, especially the genius of Stan with whom I was in daily contact. While I felt more at ease with my tall, slender, rather awkward roommate, my plan to move in with Jimmy during the next term remained in place.

Then came the episode of the unflattering picture on the cover of the magazine. I confess that I was embarrassed when students questioned my living with such a weird-looking guy: you know the cliché, " birds of a feather flock together." Then, I became furious that so many were quick to mock his looks. Stan's reaction to this humiliating experience was amazing: he acted as if nothing had happened, no matter how he felt inside. His corps of student fans — those he helped nightly — was disgusted by all the ridicule, and we quietly discussed with one another man's inhumanity to man.

Two nights later, we were as usual seated in the chairs across from each other at the old desk doing our homework, although Stan was more likely reading a novel because he had probably finished his assignments much earlier. I had become accustomed to his non-stop reading habits, his expressionless concentration. Strange how this quiet man of seventeen going on forty had such a soothing effect on my nerves. I looked up and said, "Stan, it's too much bother moving in with Jimmy next semester. Besides, I wouldn't trust anyone else with the secrets of my love life or what little there is of it. Would you mind if we continued being roommates?"

He placed the book carefully down and looked up with a lugubrious expression.

"But Ed, isn't Jim your best friend? You'll probably enjoy living with him. You've already planned it."

"I know, but I'm kind of used to you. You're a good influence. I hope you wouldn't mind if we stayed together."

Stan broke into a half smile, stood up, walked around the desk, and placed his arm on my shoulder. Then a broad smile broke over his face. "That would make me happy. Now, should we go over to Art's room and have some liverwurst and crackers?"

I never realized until later in life how important a decision I had made that night, how beneficial Stan's presence was to my future. My world opened up to new excitement in cultural matters; my mind was exposed to exceptional intellectual stimulation. I raised my scholastic sights, I strived to do better, to keep up as much as possible to Stan's accomplishments. I thrived in this climate of excellence.

Later, I was elected to Phi Beta Kappa. Down the road, I taught economics at a university, embarked on a successful career in finance.

Stan surprised everyone who did not know him. For example,

he won the affection of the most beautiful girl in the pre-med class to the envy of all of her potential boyfriends. I am certain their two-year relationship was more fulfilling socially and sexually than the few relationships that I had!

We remained good friends, but never hell-raising buddies. He was just too solid, too serious, too reserved to spend Saturday nights downtown at the favorite off-campus beer joint. When he transferred to Bowman Gray Medical School at Wake Forest in Winston-Salem (the Duke Med College had turned down his application), I missed him greatly. We, of course, kept in touch through a lively correspondence. He graduated first in his class at medical school, he went on to become a prominent doctor in New York City, and was elected in later life to the presidency of a prestigious medical society in America.

That terrible picture on the front cover of the school magazine no longer haunts me, although I can still remember the pain I felt so many years ago. How fortunate that I awakened to recognize my lucky fate to be matched with Stan. He proved to be an inspiration, a role model, and an important factor in helping me achieve many of my goals.

In later life, our career paths took us in different directions, and since we lived so far apart, we rarely reunited. Spiritually, however, we remained close.

A few years ago, a short notice that appeared in the Duke Alumni publication revealing the death of Stan after a heart attack stunned me. It was such a modest, low-key announcement, and as I grieved his passing, I realized that everything about my friend had always been modest and unassuming. In his own way, he had made his contribution to making this a better world.

VI

About the Good War

The Mustang

"Feed 'em steak and eggs. It's an old navy tradition before battle. It'll probably be the last meal for a lot of them." The skipper's smirk annoyed me on that day before our first invasion. Food was the last thing on the minds of the two hundred army combat troops aboard our ship who were sweating out the impending beachhead invasion. As it turned out, many men the next day went straight from the mess hall to the sides of the ship to disgorge their breakfasts into the sea below.

Too nervous to eat, I sipped coffee in the officers' dining room while the skipper barked out orders to remind the six young officers of their specific duties during the dangerous work ahead. Captain Allen relished his meal, no fear in his demeanor. He appeared confident and in control.

The captain dominated so much of my thinking in those days. The image of his face—leathery, deeply creased from too much sun, beady, bloodshot eyes, thin lips, and an aquiline nose— remains in my mind. He was tall, angular with a swaggering gait, in his mid-fifties. From the very beginning, he antagonized me with his critical and demanding tongue, his tone of voice when he addressed us. However, he never used cuss words. I wondered if he scorned us because we had completed college while he had to graduate from the school of hard knocks. There was no Naval Academy training in his background: he had worked his way up the naval ladder from apprentice seaman to the spot promotion of Lieutenant, U.S. Navy, in command of our LST, Landing Ship for Tanks, or as we called it, Large Slow Target.

I tried to escape his control after a few months at sea. Our

111

meeting took place in his cabin, an immaculate room lined with manuals and books about the sea, a photo of his wife on his desk, several naval citations and awards adorning his bulkheads.

The conversation was brief.

"Captain, I'd like a transfer to another ship or to different duty. I'm not happy in my present spot."

His stare was cold. After a few agonizing seconds, he snarled, "If I arrange your transfer, I shall attach an Unsatisfactory Fitness Report to go with your records. It will blemish your record forever."

"You can't do that. You know I'm doing a good job."

"That's beside the point. Your request for a transfer would make me look bad. I don't want any negatives on my file."

I dropped my request and decided to live with my discontent..

During that first invasion at Zamboanga, Mindanao, the Philippines, the captain earned my respect. He maneuvered the LST skillfully toward the beach, avoiding incoming shells, which were being lobbed in from nearby hills at the thirty-six ships moving in formation toward the landing area. One shell did hit our main deck near my stateroom, penetrating the heavy steel and lodging into the cargo area in the tank deck. Fortunately, the incoming shell severed a water main, and the water from the broken main doused the fire started by the hit. It was a lucky break for the entire operation because if our ship, loaded with inflammable material, had blown up, our companion ships on the beachhead next to us would have also exploded. As the bow plowed on to the sand and coral of the beach shoreline and the bow doors opened, two other shells ripped into the area of the landing. We learned that four of our men plus several soldiers assigned to unload the barrels of high-octane gasoline and stacks of ammunition were killed. Panic developed among the men at the scene, and they cowered on the nearby sand and in the interior of the LST.

It was a critical moment for the operation because the soldiers already ashore needed the supplies for the inland battle, and no one was unloading the cargo. Captain Allen came running in a red-faced rage, brandishing a loaded pistol and waving it at the nearby troops who were lying face-down in the forward part of the tank deck and on the shore a few yards away. The captain screamed: the veins in his neck protruded; his eyes gleamed, almost popping from their sockets. "Get back to your job of getting these supplies ashore. I'll kill anyone who shirks his responsibility."

The skipper meant it. And as the commanding officer aboard the ship, he was in control of the life and death of every person on the vessel. He was like a wild man.

The men jumped up and began working feverishly, officers included. The work lasted all day and into the night. Miraculously, no new shells hit this particular landing area, and the necessary unloading was completed.

Months later, Captain Allen received a citation for bravery under fire.

When the war finally ended, there was jubilation among almost all of the men, especially the naval reserve personnel, with beer running freely and whooping and yelling piercing the air.

The skipper was standing alone on the conning tower with tears running down his cheeks. His career advancement was about to end. No chance now for promotion to Lieutenant Commander or Full Commander. No more honors and glory. No more lording over the men. His life would be downhill from then on.

A beach setting, a few yards from the invasion site, often resurfaces in my mind. There are a few palm trees standing in an area untouched by the chaos of war three days earlier. There are forty or fifty men bowing solemnly near a freshly dug gravesite listening as the captain reads from the Bible. On the day before, at the early morning muster with the battle won and the beachhead secure, it was discovered that one more of our men was missing of the 105-man crew. A search party ashore had found the two halves of the body of our chief engineer lying in a secluded spot. A shell had gone right through his body. His wife and four children would never see him again.

The crusty skipper, acting as chaplain at the service, was sobbing uncontrollably while reading from the Good Book. I turned away from this martinet. I could not look at him as the tears welled up in my eyes, and my heart ached relentlessly.

I realized then that I did not know Captain Allen. I never knew him.

Local Students to Go to College Soon

High School days in Poughkeepsie, N.Y., saw the founding of the DSP.

Second row, first on the left with the Duke University baseball team.

Though I survived service in the war unscathed, my new bride Gloria's photo in my stateroom took some shrapnel during our first invasion.

The crew of LST 591—WW II—assembled in Evansville, Indiana, where the ship was launched.

The Pacific Odyssey of Eddie Polokoff, rendered in words and pictures.

E. Howard H. Roth, mentor to many future Merrill Leaders. Tough but fair.

Attending the Partner's Meeting of Merrill Lynch, 1959. EP can be found off on the side, near the window.

EP selling the Buffalo
Philharmonic Orchestra,
also stocks and bonds, in 1973.

With Michael Tilson Thomas,
then conductor of the Buffalo
Philharmonic, whose star rose.

While some stars subsequently fell.

Buffalo Bills ex-quarterback Jack Kemp never made
the White House (with EP and Scott Umstead).

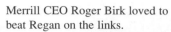

Merrill CEO Roger Birk loved to
beat Regan on the links.

Merrill CEO Donald Regan, later
member of the Reagan White House.

Bob Farrell, rated #1 market
technician for 17 consecutive years.

Merrill CEO Bill Schreyer—the
greatest people person EP ever knew.

Feted at farewell retirement party by John Steffens, Bill
Schreyer, CEO Dave Komansky and secret weapon.

Playing jazz piano at a benefit for the arts.

With wife Gina at the Great Wall.

On the road to Ephesus, Turkey, with John and Evelyn Ting, frequent traveling companions.

In the shadow of the onion domes, St. Petersburg, Russia.

Cruising the Mediterranean aboard the *Sea Cloud*.

Among the Great Pyramids.

Forbidden City? Says Who!?

Eddie—ready for the Serengeti.

With my children, front,
from left to right,
Gail, Linda and Mark

Discipline

I still remember the Captain's words: "You're becoming too friendly with the men. In a crunch, that could be dangerous. Familiarity breeds contempt."

What does he know, I figured. He barely finished high school. I was an honor graduate from a quality university. The only thing he knew anything about was the regular navy. Most of his former shipmates had little education, came from tough backgrounds, knew little about leadership. At least, that's how I analyzed the situation.

Aboard our ship, which operated in the Pacific Theater during World War II, I was the youngest of the nine officers and one of the youngest of the one hundred ten-man crew. My quick smile made me a favorite among the enlisted men; there was always the friendly greeting, "How's your wife? How's the world treating you?"

The skipper frowned when he heard me call Kovaleski, "Wally"—a man I treated more like a friend than a subordinate. This approach put me at ease. I wanted to be regarded as one of the guys, not a college-kid snob.

The captain kept haranguing me, "You need their respect, not their love. You need their obedience. They must never question your authority."

My personality concealed the scars from prejudice and anti-semitism. The lonely hours I had spent as a youth fighting tears because of slurs made in my presence about Jews, the fist fights with bullies who picked on me because of my religion. It was no wonder that I had established a defense mechanism embracing the idea that if people liked me enough, the Jew-baiting would end.

I had turned to sports as an antidote. My mother would stick her head out the back door and shout through the dusk blanketing my neighborhood, "Eddy. Your dinner is getting cold. Get in here."

Every late afternoon I would be across the street in the park practicing baseball, football, tennis, basketball until it was too dark to see.

"Why are you so *meshuganeh* about sports?"

I explained to her that I didn't like the reputation that Jews had as not being athletes. They were labeled "bookworms." I vowed to excel in the gentile world as an athlete. It would be one way to win approval, to gain acceptance as a different kind of Jew.

My heroes were the home-run slugger of the Detroit Tigers, Hank Greenberg, and the great pitcher of the Dodger team, Sandy Koufax, who wouldn't pitch in the World Series on Yom Kippur. Other Jews like Benny Goodman, the jazz musician, and Albert Einstein, the genius scientist, were my idols. FDR did not make my popularity list. Did he help the Jews against Hitler? No.

The carryover shame was with me in the navy.

"What kind of name is Polokoff, sir?"

"Russian," I replied.

Why didn't I say "Jewish?"

I was still battling feelings of insecurity, inferiority. No doubt, behind my back, the men figured it out by themselves, called me the "kike" or "Jew-boy." So, I would be a nice guy. They would like me.

The skipper knew better.

"Keep your distance."

My leadership style appeared to work. The men carried out my orders, not questioning my judgement. Wally balked now and then, good-naturedly resisting my directions. I made no fuss about his contrariness. Once, I did step down on him.

"Aw, Mr. Polokoff, I'm too tired today to do the inventory. I'll do it tomorrow."

I stared angrily.

"You'll do it today."

"Aw, shit. Well, okay."

He slouched away, a scowl over his eyes.

Life aboard ship, in most cases, was a monotonous, repetitious flow of events. Reveille, muster, chow, work details, chow, work details, battle condition drills, chow, over and over again. There were the four hours on, eight hours off duty shifts for manning and maintaining the ship plus the rotational shore leave for the men while in port. Preparation for battle conditions was an ongoing routine day after day on an LST (Landing Ship—Tanks) even though actual involvement in invasions occurred infrequently. Many evenings, when off duty, I would be an isolated figure standing near the bow of the ship, viewing the orangey sky at sunset while listening to the strains of *Scheherazade* flowing over the public address system, wondering about my fate, wondering if I would ever return to the States alive and in one piece.

A quiet day at sea was shattered one afternoon by the shriek of the general quarters siren accompanied by the frantic bellowing voice over the public address speaker.

"General quarters. Man your battle stations. This is not a drill. Torpedoes sighted off starboard bow."

Then ensued the wild scrambling of the men to different parts of the ship according to prearranged assignments. Excitement and fear were partners in the exercise. The responses to the danger were automatic.

I was in charge of the stern battle detail consisting of twenty men of my division, all gathered awaiting my orders to confront possible emergencies in that part of the ship.

"Burke, Owens, Sanders. Rush up forward to help the spotters there," I ordered.

I knew there were but few men assigned to that section of the ship.

"You shouldn't do that, Mr. Polokoff. Our assignment is that we all stay together here at the stern."

The men stared at Kovaleski; a few seemed confused, rattled by his outburst.

"One more comment like that, Kovaleski, and you're in the brig."

The three men, reassured by my firmness, responded, "Aye, aye, sir."

They ran toward their new station.

Flushed and scared, we all scanned the surrounding waters watching for other torpedoes. The captain commenced maneuvering the ship in a zigzag formation so that we would not be an easy target. We heard an explosion on the ship abreast of us about five hundred yards away. Almost instantly, that LST broke in half and began sinking. In about eleven seconds, the ship disappeared completely. We looked vainly for heads bobbing in the water; there were no survivors.

"Stay alert, men. Watch for submarines or torpedoes in the area," I commanded.

Two more torpedoes whizzed by about twenty yards off our rear. The frightening encounters lasted no more than five minutes. Fortunately, only one ship was hit of the thirty-six LSTs in the flotilla.

We watched the destroyer escorts, destroyers, patrol boats combing the sea looking for submarines. We heard the staccato of depth charges exploding in the water seeking out the enemy sub. No hits. The enemy had escaped. Well into the night, we remained at battle alert. All of the next day, our armada of ships continued on their routes—using the zigzag evasive formations. The attacking sub or subs were never discovered. The serenity of the Pacific returned. The contrast between the sight of ships in perfect formation gliding over the placid ocean and the always-present danger of lurking submarines was a striking reminder of how close death can be to life in wartime.

The transition from being Mr. Nice Guy to Mr. Heavy was not

easy. I had spent so many weeks cultivating good feelings with the men, and suddenly, I had to become a strict "by the book" officer who entertained no small talk, who became a stickler for detail, who expected complete obedience and respect. Wally was now Kovaleski at every encounter; he seemed baffled by my personality change. He no longer liked me, a consequence to my earlier flawed leadership approach. My relationships with the other members of the crew deteriorated into moody sullenness on their part. I sacrificed popularity for the need for discipline. But I did end up a more effective officer.

Inexplicable

My reflections on the "Good War" are less about a hostile sea tossing our fragile LST around in the South Pacific; are less about the thunderous bombardments of the beachheads before invasions at Leyte, Mindanao, and Borneo. They are more about the way fate played a part in the shaping of a young life thrown into the maelstrom of war.

How odd that my orders were changed to report to Notre Dame Midshipmen School at South Bend instead of Northwestern Midshipmen School at Chicago, the original destination, on the day when we departed the Norfolk Training Base for officer training.

Upon arrival in a mist at the train station at South Bend, I was met, by chance, by Lieutenant Ben Smith, formerly a close acquaintance at Duke University. He was the officer in charge of handling the incoming group of a hundred potential officers.

"Hi, Eddy. What a small world to see you here."

"Hello, Sir. Happy to see a familiar face." I was keeping my proper distance from a superior officer.

With a smile, he said, "There are a lot of attractive gals around here. Just remember that about a third of the incoming sailors end up marrying South Bend girls."

"Come on. That's impossible. How can a guy meet a girl, then marry her inside of ninety days?"

"I'm just stating facts."

Shortly thereafter, I met my wife-to-be. We were married four months later.

This never could have happened if I had gone to Northwestern instead of Notre Dame.

This wartime love affair glued me to the Notre Dame scene. Halfway through the training period, the arches in my feet broke down, and the resultant pain was so acute that I could not participate in the marching and exercise program required for the curriculum. Under normal circumstances, I might have requested transfer to the Japanese language school at Denver since I had been an honor student in languages; or I might have been discharged because of a physical disability. But I was in love. I didn't want to leave Notre Dame. Ben Smith came to the rescue when I sought his help.

"Go to this foot doctor downtown. I hear he is a genius with problems like yours."

I rushed to the specialist, he fitted me with arch supports, and I was able to participate in the required physical activities. The doctors in sick bay on the base had been unable to help me in my crisis. Who knows how my life would have veered had not that doctor been able to fix my flat feet problem?

Then there was the strange sequence of events during our first invasion. I had made a quick stop at the "head" in my stateroom ten seconds earlier when an incoming shell, fired from a big gun ashore, exploded in my room, destroying almost everything in my quarters. That particular shell also penetrated the deck in my room and lodged in the tank deck below, and in so doing, busted the water pipe, flooding the immediate area. A fire had broken out because of the explosion in the cargo area, but the rush of water from the severed pipe doused the flames. The cargo included large supplies of high-octane gas and ammunition, which certainly would have blown up without the flood of water. Furthermore, it is possible that the other thirty-five ships sitting side-by-side on the beach would have caught on fire, jeopardizing the entire assault force.

My LST, the 591, was damaged so severely in the invasion of Mindanao, the Philippines, that the ship was dispatched to Leyte harbor for extensive repairs. How ironic that while we were sitting out of harm's way in dry-dock, we were spared participating in two exceptionally dangerous operations, the assault on Iwo Jima and later, the invasion of Okinawa where the Japanese Kamikaze suicide pilots destroyed several hundred American ships.

These unusual circumstances are inexplicable.

VII

About Travel

An American in Chelsea

Chelsea is overflowing with young, tall, shapely girls wearing tight-fitting skirts and slacks, platform shoes, show-all bras or no bras. Boobs are in—and often out—with all ages of women showing off their personal best. Crazy hair styles and wild hair colors among younger men and women create additional incentives for people watching. Adding to the zaniness is the pierced everything craze—noses, navels, ears, toes, stomachs with weird types of decorative jewelry protruding from the pierced areas. King's Row, the main and bustling artery and the birthplace of the miniskirt craze in the sixties, reminded us of Yorkville in Toronto. There is a League of Nations mixture of people on the streets in both cities.

As American tourists living in Chelsea for two months, we found that the attraction of our small apartment with its living room-dining room combination, tiny kitchen, small bathroom, and bedroom was its location, walking distance to almost every important activity in London. Many good restaurants are no more than thirty or forty minutes walk away. We always enjoyed the walks both ways, but for non-walkers, the famous London cabbies are readily available at reasonable prices, usually between five and ten dollars per fare. These drivers proffer a polite and smiling "Thank you," whether you tip them or not. Food costs about the same as in the States. Sea bass and Dover sole are specialties; rack of lamb is usually excellent. La Tante Claire, Gordon Ramsey, Connaught Grill, Poissonerie de l'Avenue are among the dozens that merit New York City ranking. For lunch, fish soup is featured at the pubs and brassieres; unfortunately, French fries weigh down too many menus, but you don't have to eat them all.

Pubs are a growth business, except that there are no free corners left to locate new ones. Beer runs freely side by side with good-natured conversation and the ever-present cigarette smoke. The anti-smoking drive has by-passed England. Everybody seems to be lighting up.

Flowers abound in all directions. It is impossible to walk without running into small parks bordering the streets with views of columns of roses, peonies, azaleas, delphiniums, and on and on. Then there are the giant parks, geography book famous, such as Hyde Park, St. James Park, Kew Gardens, Regency Park, to name a few, acres of lush land with lakes, trees, fields for games, walking areas, benches, floral paths, manicured gardens and their treasuries of verdant plants and blossoming flowers. Each park seems joined together with the next huge one like in a majestic symphonic progression. Blending in to this color parade are row upon row of apartment buildings bedecked with flowering arrangements on the ledges of windows; each resident is intent on beautifying his little domain as a challenge to his neighbor. Private homes are jeweled by the same pattern of meticulous garden and floral settings. Even neighborhood churches, ancient and austere in concrete with their spires, join into the panoply of colorful display. Gracing the church courtyards are beds with yellow, red, white, purple varieties offering parishioners a peaceful alternative to attending formal service. The pious might feel closer to God sitting on the benches along the paths meditating about the flowers than listening to a sermon inside about social issues.

In addition, spread throughout the city are the stalls of vendors on the streets, often no more than six blocks apart, each vendor offering his array of flowers, often exotic, whether calla lilies, birds of paradise, or poppies. These merchants do a non-stop business from mid-morning to dinnertime. The familiar sight along King's Road is of many people hastening along the street carrying grocery bags along with their bouquets for home. The fragrance from the booths is intoxicating as you stroll past.

As to the weather, we found June and July fine. Not too sweltering hot as you might find in Florida or most states—although there were two consecutive 90 degree days—and not too cool. A range between 64 and 74 is commonplace, but carrying a "brelly" is practical because of the unpredictability of light drizzle popping up due to the nearness of ocean breezes. London is unfairly cursed about its climate; the weather is similar to that in Northern Europe.

The press and television are amusingly critical of just about everything. Of the one hundred thirty-six shows running in the theater district—walking distance from Chelsea, the critics have grudging praise for but few of them. Sports commentators are brutal in sizing up performance of the stars; it is refreshing when they don't fawn. In tennis, comments like, "Maybe Tim Henman needs a new coach to get him to the next level." Or, "The English didn't come to play tennis today."

In football, "England was terrible, doesn't belong in World Cup Championship play. So-and-so suffered a stupid penalty which cost us the crucial match."

The commentators are as much fun as the competitions.

Politicians take a drubbing too. Prime Minister Tony Blair is a favorite target, and when his sixteen-year-old son was arrested for being drunk in a public square, Blair had to endure the wrath of the press. The comment was made, "After thirty-one consecutive bad days, this is Blair's worst."

A popular morning TV talk show is hosted by a Mr. Kilroy, a former Member of Parliament steeped in British respectability. He is an affable, smooth operator handling such titillating topics, such as, "I want to sleep with my best friend's wife." Or, "How many times a week do you want sex with your mate or anyone?"

The English seem to have a fixation about sex. (Well, maybe Americans do too.) What other conclusion would you come to when you read the lead story in a popular entertainment magazine, *Time Off*, entitled, "Summer Sex," which describes the ten best places in London for random intercourse, including the Dome, the

Tate Modern Gallery, the Mayfair Club? Another piece reveals tricks for girls to use to achieve orgasm with specific reference to super effective vibrators. The F-word is an "in" expression in this publication, but there is little discussion about morality. Are the young people waging guerrilla warfare against establishment Brits with their stiff upper lips or is it just a sign of general deterioration of the code of sexual behavior in England and worldwide?

World attention has focused on the recently completed Tate Modern Museum; it is only a hop-skip-and-jump from Chelsea because of a free bus service from the nearby old Tate Museum on the Thames River. A former power plant was converted into this architectural phenomenon at a cost of one hundred forty-three million dollars; it is five hundred feet long and one hundred seventy-five feet high. The five-story-high structure houses some of the most unusual works of modern art and sculpture in the world. The old Tate itself is a treasure house of the Masters with the large Turner collection of watercolors impressive. Add the National Gallery at Trafalgar Square, also available by free bus, and the Victoria and Albert Museum at High Park, and a strong case can be made that Chelsea is the perfect starting point to the greatest collection of art in the world.

The Royal Chelsea Hospital for retired pensioners is worth a visit. A chat with some of the retired soldiers is revealing. There are three hundred sixty-six in residence, all single, all enthusiastic about their quarters, the food, their lifestyle. If they decide to leave the facility, they go back on pension; while there, they give up their pension. Very few ever leave. They walk the streets of Chelsea, uniformed neatly, always available to talk about their wartime experiences with eyes glistening as they relive their close calls and memorable duty in faraway places like Singapore, Burma, or Egypt. The complex itself, located on a two mile square tract graced with gardens, woods, walking areas, contains a group of dormitories, a chapel, the paneled Great Dining Hall, a clinic, and open spaces of land converted annually into the famous Chelsea

Garden Show. This show is overattended by thousands of garden and plant lovers at a fancy admission charge. The demand is so great that we were unable to buy tickets.

Whether you wander along the nearby Thames or explore mammoth Harrods, you always feel that you must return again soon. Next time, you'll spend more time in upscale Mayfair with its tony stores and boutiques. It's only a few blocks away and a worthwhile reason to vacation over the pond once more.

Return to Kenya?

In order to break up the long flight from Kennedy International to Nairobi via Europe, we stopped over in Amsterdam for a six-hour rest at an airport hotel. We had originally planned to nap for a few hours, but we decided to rent a car and driver to tour the city, especially the famous red light district. It was a cold, rainy night and worse, a foolish venture: viewing scantily clad girls sitting in storefront windows with cigarettes dangling from their lips was more a dismal sight than a turn-on for tourists. This diversion brought us running noses when we resumed our flight to Nairobi. My discomfort from snuffing and sneezing increased, and in addition, I sensed a urinary infection developing. I learned later that quinine tablets suggested for travelers to Kenya occasionally aggravate prostate problems.

After many years of looking forward to this trip, I fretted about how poorly things were starting out. I snapped back to enthusiasm once we soaked in the flavors of Nairobi with its mixture of ancient bazaars and modern hotels and buildings, the old and the new. After a couple of days of orientation, we embarked with a small safari group on a trip to the game lodges in the interior of the country in a sturdy Land Rover manned by a native driver and a guide. I remained concerned about the possibility of a urinary blockage similar to the one that had hit me a few years earlier, but I hoped my nervousness would subside. It didn't.

Our first stop was at the Lodge at Tsavo Game Park, and at about midnight, my anxiety increased because symptoms of a potential blockage appeared. My previous experience with this condition had led to such excruciating pain that dying seemed almost preferable to suffering until a catheter had relieved the pressure. We awakened the guide to alert him to my predicament, we reviewed the potential danger to my health in such a remote area, and we decided to drive back to Nairobi for an emergency hospital examination. By 2:00 A.M. we were packed and ready to go in the Rover back to the city, a four-hour ride.

"We can't go yet. We must wait till dawn. It is too dangerous now," the driver and the guide both announced.

"Are the animals such a threat?" I asked.

"No, the poachers are out there now. If they run into us, they will kill us. They want no witnesses to their illegal activities!"

I worried about a two- or three-hour delay, imagining the pain that could occur if a blockage did indeed take place. At last, a pale yellowy dawn broke over the landscape, and we sped off on the lonely macadam road toward Nairobi after first leaving an explanatory note for the other members of the party.

My near panic gradually diminished as we bathed in the early morning beauty of the Kenyan plains. There were hundreds of animals wandering around the road—elephants, zebras, buffalo, wildebeest, lions, hyenas, vultures, almost every species imaginable. They offered no threat to us as long as we ignored them. Fortunately, there were no poachers around. The journey was one of those rare travel experiences that one can never forget—with the famous snow-capped Mount Kilimanjaro staring down upon us from a distance. My wife, Gina, and I later agreed that the best animal viewings are in the early morning, not during the heat of day when the game are sleeping or wandering around lazily.

Once in the city, we became more relaxed about my medical condition. Our spirits soared as we contemplated professional attention at the large, modern hospital. Jeb, our handsome, articulate, ebony black guide—movie star material, we decided—took us to the emergency clinic. Our driver reluctantly left us in order to return to the others in the safari group for the continuation of their adventure. He seemed so anxious that the doctor would give me clearance to join up later with our group.

In spite of Jeb's commanding presence, we received no special attention at the hospital as we stood in line for well over an hour in a first-come, first-served setup. It was a remarkable scene—a kaleidoscope in color—with people of different shades of skin, speaking various dialects and from all stages of the economic ladder, wearing mostly wildly bright clothing. Gina whispered about the noticeable lack of cleanliness at the medical facility, and as we viewed the blood bank room adjacent to the waiting area, we discussed quietly the theory prevalent in those days that AIDS had originated in Kenya!

Finally, I was ushered into a curtained private space where a young female intern, by appearance Indian born, interviewed me. She was sorry, but she had little expertise in the field of urology. She would happily turn me over to a urologist, but it was his day off. Jeb remained polite, but angry because we were unable to obtain prompt attention. Fortunately, we were able to check in to an excellent hotel for the night. Jeb arranged an appointment for me the next day with a urologist of excellent reputation. I telephoned my doctor back in the States (surprising that we got through in a couple of seconds), and he suggested some band-aid type treatment which proved useful.

A good meal plus a fine bottle of wine at the Norfolk Hotel helped the evening pass quickly, and the Valium recommended by my doctor gave me a good night's sleep. The next morning at the office of the urologist proved to be a welcome tonic to my morale because this competent doctor with the clipped English accent provided reassuring words and the proper pills to treat my minor infection. The next day, I felt fine.

Secure in our confidence in the doctor's prognosis of my condition, we arranged transportation to the game park lodge, the famous Treetops, where the rest of our party was scheduled for arrival that day.

We arrived at Treetops at dusk, just in time, because once

darkness settles in, the vertical wooden structure becomes inaccessible with the numerous animals completely surrounding the building. Indeed, guests at the lodge become prisoners for the night. We climbed the ladder to the top of the platform on which dining, viewing, and bedroom facilities rested. Our safari friends gave us a big cheer as we reached the landing. The magnet at Treetops was the huge watering hole one hundred feet to one side of the square building. Long into the night and well past midnight, we viewed from the balcony the different animals making their appearances at the water for drinking and bathing. A spotlight focused on the two-hundred-foot long lake. The wild creatures were fascinating to watch, but the thirty-one elephants dominated the show as they marched in procession to the water for their antics, including fornication with bellowing grunts.

We had learned at dinner that night about native lore: there is this superstition that a safari group is jinxed if any member of the group drops out for whatever reason. It was only then that we fully understood why everyone had been so joyful once we reunited with the group.

There were numerous thrills during the remaining nine days of the expedition; we brought back many stories about the unique adventure. While my health returned to normal, Gina labored under a severe bronchial infection which hung on stubbornly until we returned to the United States. Kenya was exciting, but the glamorous aspects remain tainted by some negative memories.

Would we go again? Avid travelers are always weighing the excitement of exotic experiences compared to the discomforts of hectic airports, crowded airplanes, and other assorted problems. On balance, getting there is usually worth the inconveniences.

After Kenya, I'm not so keen for a journey to a place like Nepal, for example. Cap Ferrat on the French Riviera seems more enticing!

VIII

About Musings

Where Have You Gone, Joe DiMaggio?

I miss baseball.

When I was a kid, it was my life. I played or practiced every day for ten years, except when the snow was thick on the ground or the temperature was below freezing.

I knew every team in the American League and every team in the National League—all sixteen of them. I studied the box scores of each major league game as a daily chore of love. I could rattle off the names of the players and their batting averages, pitching records, interesting statistics about their careers. I idolized my favorites—PeeWee Reese, Ted Williams, Joe DiMaggio, Willy Mays, Sandy Koufax, and forty or fifty others. They weren't just stars; they were family. I rooted with fervor for my team, the underdog Brooklyn Dodgers, and for my hero, Joe DiMaggio, season after season. I could depend on DiMaggio being on the same team in the same lineup every day year after year. Living or dying with my team and my hero became a ritual. My vicarious thrills came from the box scores. Girls and sex came in a distant second. That's how it was some forty, fifty years ago.

Today, the game still exists, but not for me.

I never go to a game, care little about any team, am not interested in any player, will watch possibly a bit of the final game of the World Series on television.

I recognize that baseball players are skillful athletes, and I could enjoy watching them perform as exhibitionists, not as members of a team. How can I establish an attachment for a team when its personnel is changing so frequently, when its home base might be Brooklyn one year, Los Angeles the next year?

How can I hero-worship players of average talent earning three or four million a year? With free agency in effect, they might make tons more skipping from one team to another. I can not fault an athlete for preferring to play for ten million a year instead of four million, but I can wonder about his sense of team loyalty and his loyalty to his fans.

The average fan is plunking down a lot of hard-earned money to cheer for, in too many cases, players who often become prima donnas on the baseball diamond. Occasionally, I am willing to pay the steep admission fee to see a rock star perform, but that rare indulgence will not damage my budget. Attending many baseball games (or exhibitions, I call them) can wreck the family finances.

Baseball was fun in the old days when I followed religiously my team and my hero, Joe DiMaggio, whether they won or lost. It was a game then. It is big business now.

I miss baseball.

Falling Leaves

Inexorably, my old gang of family, close friends, and clients appears to be disappearing. Solitary leaves are drifting down from the solid oak tree in a desultory pattern. The tree is slowly thinning.

There was my dad, sturdy and strong, who rarely was ill, who surrendered to bladder cancer in his late seventies. In retrospect, had he not been so stubborn—or was he afraid to know—in not heeding the ominous warnings of blood in his urine, he might have been successfully treated for his ailment. Instead, he had to bear the shame and pain of walking around the room feebly with the IV solutions feeding into his frail body at the end.

Mother did well into her nineties, but the last ten years were plagued with bad legs, hips, lungs, and mostly loneliness, bitterness and hopelessness as her time ran out, and she finally just gave in.

My piano-playing partner from Duke, Art Bauer, synonymous with Count Basie, Duke Ellington, and Teddy Wilson, retired early to North Carolina, enjoyed a few good years; then, all kinds of cancer devoured him. I'll always regret ignoring his gentle hint in a letter, "You better come down to visit this disappearing man. I'd love to see you." Little did I realize that he was trying to warn me without alarming me. Such was this sweet man.

Stan Wallace, college roommate, genius, rock-solid friend, inspirational role model, died as anonymously as he wanted to live, excepting that he left behind his marks as one of the top arthritis specialists in America, as the president of a prestigious medical society in New York City. Always a modest man, he showed the way by example and straightened me out into someone worthwhile.

E. Howard H. Roth I can never forget, and a full, fruitful life he led. He milked every bit of joy out of his ninety-one years with three wives (I dare not speculate on the number of sexual liaisons), enormous wealth and power, many lives full of travel, adventure, and success. He was my mentor who guided me to wealth at Merrill Lynch, and I learned volumes from him about how to live and how not to live.

Joe Steinmetz was one of my closest colleagues at Merrill Lynch. A husky, overweight, elfish, smiling man of ordinary ability, average intelligence, a remarkable talent for sales, extraordinary friendliness to all people, Joe was older but young. He died in his eighties, a prosperous man with a fine family, oodles of friends, who told boring stories, which were sometimes funny. How he lasted as long as he did always amazed me when I consider all the cigars he smoked, all the sausage and eggs and beef he ate, all the manhattans and martinis he drank, all the non-exercise he did, all the three-foot putts he missed.

Then there was Nate Rosen. Nathan Detroit, we called him, although nothing like the character in *Guys and Dolls*. Nate was a second father to my son, my accompanist on the annual father-son golf expedition with our sons each spring to Hershey or Florida or Bermuda or the Bahamas. A smart businessman, a fair to poor golfer, a lovable, overweight teddy bear, he ended up rich and powerful. But he ate too much, did not exercise, and was confident that he was indestructible, never thought he would die in the surgery he elected to have for his prostate and related problems.

Dr. Bob Warner, the pixie director of the Rehabilitation Center of the Buffalo Children's Hospital, was world famous in his field, a true humanitarian, a generous, loving man. Older, but perennially young in spirit, he put off dying until he was eighty in order to see the birth of one of his grandchildren in California. He was born into money, was a fine pediatrician upon graduation from Harvard Medical School, spent many hours sitting on our living room rug examining my babies when they were sick. Some doctors did make house calls in those days. We had enormous faith in each other's judgment, and we bathed in a close friendship until his death.

I mention Bob Millonzi, Mr. Philharmonic, a name later bestowed upon me, although he will always be the real McCoy. He brought me into the Buffalo Philharmonic family, became a good client, was a charming dilettante, a big booster. A successful lawyer dedicated to good health habits, he died suddenly and shockingly doing one of his favorite things, playing golf at the Country Club of Buffalo, at age seventy-five. No one, including him, suspected a heart condition.

Irvine Kittinger, the wasp, the gentleman, a huge client, fan and booster in the non-Jewish community, died at a comfortable old age, but not before he had sponsored me for the prestigious Buffalo Foundation, for which I served for ten years, two years as chairman. He was an elder statesman, a prince, and I loved him.

Then there was old, fat Charlie Altman, one of my first big customers, who treated me like the son he never had. Mike Kahn was a business giant and brain, a huge influence in my early career, a valuable confidant, and an advisor in my United Jewish Fund campaign. It was sad to see this powerful man with a dynamic personality wither away in an upscale Catholic nursing facility.

How depressing to reminisce about my golfing buddies, many of them from the boys' excursions to Rolling Hills in Fort Lauderdale, Florida, every winter. Stormin' Norman Lewis, competitor excellence, putter supreme, lover of steaks, always in great shape, handsome, a handball star, a supremely cocky and efficient trial lawyer, died in his sixties—another surprise because he seemed indomitable. The hero type, he stayed strong to the end.

"When did you suspect health problems?" I asked him.

"I noticed a change in my stool."

He was gone in a few months, and he wasn't a smoker.

Leo Biltekoff, so smooth and easygoing, but sharp in business, smoked and drank too much. A fine golfer, good hell raiser, he did not have an enemy in the world. Excepting cancer.

There was the Blue Sky Club, the golfing, social, and investment group, which I ran with an iron fist for twenty years. It became wildly famous in the Buffalo community, and my reputation soared because of the performance of the portfolio. Unfortunately, some great guys passed away—Koessler, Koch, Hohl, Morrison. And then more.

The thing that amazed me about one of the guys was the size of his penis. In the men's shower, we laughed and marveled about it, but he was proud. It also did plenty of duty.

Bobby Dobkin, Mr. Clean, the exercise and walking addict, father of a fine cardiologist who helped him with his heart disease, but who couldn't help him lick lung cancer, which struck quickly and fatally. He smoked when he was very young.

I recall my friend, golfing partner, good client and fine urologist, Dr. George Fugitt, who weighed close to three hundred pounds. He was the sweetest guy in the world, but he loved to eat, and he passed away in his fifties.

There are too many others. A guy like Bede Joseph never should have gone, so young in his early forties, already a community leader, a Lebanese Christian who had so much charisma. But he was macho, and he declined to undergo the surgery which would have saved his life, but which would have damaged his sexual prowess.

When my wife's mother went, it was almost a blessing because she had suffered so much with kidney failure, heart disease, and lung cancer. Still, she got five extra years in, and most of those years were enjoyable with her kids and grandkids. A remarkable event was how she held on to life until all of her loved ones had time to arrive at bedside from far-off places. Then, she let go. Gina suffered badly from the experience, still feels the loss. When Gina's mentor, Alan Chiara, died suddenly from a heart attack at age fifty-seven, that disaster knocked Gina back considerably.

A more recent loss is my buddy of years gone by, Butch Abelson. We used to raise a lot of hell together, and his infectious belly laugh was famous in Buffalo. Married late in life, he idolized his two daughters. He became closer to his wife once she was struck by cancer. She suffered and died shortly before he left, and incredibly, she had no bad health habits. Why Butch died of cancer is hard to nail down. He did not smoke, but he was a heavy drinker. On the other hand, his father lived to ninety-three, and he never stopped drinking. Butch suffered under several handicaps: he exercised little, he worked too hard, he did not vacation enough, and he was an inordinate worrier. Stress is a killer. The other night I dreamt about Butch. My dreams are usually sexually oriented. This one wasn't.

Butch was hosting a huge outdoor picnic type of party. About three hundred people were in attendance on a sparkling sunny day in the country. He looked wonderful. I walked up to him and said, "Butch, you look terrific. What a remarkable recovery. You must be okay again."

"Yeah, I'm better now." And with that attractive half grin. "I'm okay, Eddy."

Did he come back from the other side to comfort me?

Why one goes, why one stays will always be a mystery. Can bad habits predict bad ends? Can good habits fight off bad endings? There are patterns, but not reliable guidelines.

So, the strong oak tree will continue to shed its leaves, slowly and inexorably. All that we mortals can do is rely on good joss and enjoy the scene while life goes on.

Essential Edwinisms*

• Moderation in all things, including abstinence.

• Often wrong, never in doubt.

• A carrot is man's best friend.

• The secrets to good health are a good diet and a good digestive system.

• A little stress is okay A lot of stress is a killer.

• The Peter Principle is alive and well. Don't bite off more than you can chew.

• Hate is a bad word.

• When you're dead, you're dead a long time.

• Don't sweat the small stuff.

• Too many people, who are in a hurry, get to the cemetery too soon.

• Respect your mental and physical limitations.

• Long hours of uninterrupted work eventually break down the body.

- Don't talk about your age or your money.

- How old would I be if you didn't know my age?

- Don't. If you do and get in trouble, see me first.

- You can stop the mountain; you can stop the sea; but you can't stop Eddy P.

- The harder I work, the luckier I get.

- Get DDM before FU.

*But not necessarily original

The Rules of the Road for Investors*

- The darlings become the dogs; the dogs become the darlings.

- Love affairs should be reserved for marriage, not stocks.

- A common stock can become very common.

- Diversify.

- Diversify!

- The market tells its own story. It knows more than anyone.

- A dangerous prediction: stocks always come back.

- A dangerous attitude: I don't care. I can wait. I'm in it for the long term.

- Sell enough of a large position so that you can sleep well at night.

- It's a market of stocks, not a stock market.

- When you want in, buy at the market. When you want out, sell at the market. You shouldn't be concerned about quarters and halves when thousands of dollars are at stake.

- There are no geniuses in the market. A relatively few have the touch and knowledge to do better than average.

- Doing nothing is a decision, and often a bad one.

- If you are right more than sixty percent of the time, you are a genius. If you are right more than seventy-five percent of the time, you are a liar.

- Your chances of making money in the market are best when everything looks awful. Your chances of making money in the market are worst when everything looks wonderful.

- He who panics first panics best.

- Everything is price and timing on individual issues.

- Boring can be beautiful in the stock market.

- Selling is just as important as buying.

- When you make a switch, you have to be right twice.

- Never run the same horse in the next race.

- Free advice might cost you money.

- Bulls make money; bears make money; pigs don't make money in the stock market.

*But not necessarily original

IX

About EP Trying Fiction

Mei Li

Mei Li sobbed softly as she glided through the creaky wooden door at the back of the white cement block building housing the massage parlor. She dabbed her tears away, forced a faint smile as she greeted her colleagues briefly, and sat on a chair in front of a mirror as she applied a light makeup to her smooth skin.

The pleading voice of Tien Chin, her adoring Daddy, was still in her mind, "My beautiful princess is too good for such work. Quit. Find another job. Do anything else."

The shrill tone of her mother, Tu Tu, rebutting in the background, "Shut up. You brought ten kids into this world. We need the money she brings home. She can take care of herself."

Mei Li had always been Tien's favorite. She used to dress up pretty for him, do dances, flirt, and listen to his funny stories every night. Now she was fifteen with velvety light brown skin, languorous eyes, a winsome smile, jet-black hair falling to her shoulders. She felt especially beautiful, but Daddy noticed a hardening of her expression, which told pages about her work. He wished he could find better paying work than his laboring on the farm just outside of Bangkok so that Mei Li would not have to make the daily five-mile trek to the massage parlor every late afternoon. He had once dreamt that his beauty would end up the prized bride of a wealthy merchant. Such a dream seemed impossible now.

Mei Li agonized over her predicament: how to spare Tien's broken heart and satisfy Tu Tu's greed at the same time.

The squalid dressing room behind the stage was crowded with some thirty girls, aged thirteen to thirty, some plump, some thin, all attractive. They ungarbed to their panties, tied bandana-type signs with numbers on them across their breasts, and proceeded to their allotted spots on the four rows of bleachers mounted on the stage in front of an opaque mirror. Prospective clients could look in; the girls could not see out. After a year at the massage parlor, Mei Li no longer dreaded the business at hand in spite of realizing that the bizarre arrangement bore a similarity to a slave-labor auction.

Men standing on the other side of the window could peer at the display of girls, make their selections by use of the numbers across the bosoms. Mei Li was usually the first or second to be chosen. She played her nightly mind game: would he be young or old, muscular or flabby, an American sailor or an Australian soldier, a German businessman or an English tourist, a brute with liquor on his breath or an aesthete reeking with perfume. Maybe, like in the movies, Prince Charming would fall in love with her and rescue her from this tawdry existence.

Mr. Supanee, a slight, middle-aged man with dull eyes and a cigarette dangling from his narrow lips, had been supervising the selection process. As usual, Mei Li was quickly chosen. Supanee slipped behind the bleachers, beckoned Mei Li, led her through the dimly lit corridor to Room 1 a few yards away.

As she entered the dreary room, she paid scant attention to the man standing barefooted next to the mattress-sized inflated rubber mat centered on the concrete deck in the fourteen by fourteen-foot cubicle. She walked directly to the bucket of warm water and plastic container of liquid soap near the mat, doused the furrowed rubber bed with water and then soap, scrubbed down the mat, creating a slippery film on top of the bed. Finally, she gazed wanly toward the customer who was wearing an awkward smile. The scene was cold: the sole piece of furniture was a wooden chair in the corner. Two terry cloth towels draped loosely over the back of the chair. The frosted light bulb protruding from a socket in the ceiling cast a bleak, yellowy light into the room.

Exhibiting a coquettish grin as she established eye contact with the young man, she moved over in front of him and began removing his clothes very slowly. First, she unbuttoned his khaki sport shirt and slid it off. Then she unzipped the fly on his tight-fitting slacks and slipped the pants down and off. Finally, she pulled down and off his jockey shorts. For a moment, she was startled: the man was blond, muscular, well-proportioned with a hairy chest— quite a contrast from the usual client. Soaping him down was pleasurable.

"Lie down on your back," she whispered.

She slid off her panties, removed the bandana-type brassiere from her small, but firm breasts, then lay down beside him and maneuvered her legs over and under his waist. She proceeded with her routine of sliding her arms, hands, legs all over his form, careful to avoid direct contact with his eager erection. Somehow, during the year of employment, she had managed to avoid coitus during the hour period of eroticism. Most times, the massage was a mask for sexual stimulation. Often, an early ejaculation would end the session, the customer's interest would wane, and the twenty-dollar fee was earned quickly. This night would become increasingly trying for Mei Li because the customer was attractive and shyly engaging, and she had difficulty ignoring the powerfully erect penis.

Tien Chin's voice, usually in her memory, seemed dimmer this night. Mr. Supanee's entreating pleas were ringing through her mind as she slithered over the body of the handsome mate.

"Make them happy. You are so beautiful that it will be over in a minute. You will get so rich so fast. You can keep half of what they give you extra. Work full time for me. Live in the dormitory with the other girls. Forget that long walk back and forth to your house. You're a big girl now. You can take care of yourself."

Suddenly, strange emotions converged on her brain—as if a psychedelic mist had clouded around her. There followed a quickened heartbeat, a burst of erotic arousal. Mei Li closed her eyes, drifted into a trance, all weak from toes to the tip of her head. Almost unconsciously, she groped for his steel-like rod, then seized it firmly and directed it toward her personal treasure.

"Please. Make love to me. I know you do not believe me, but it will be my first time."

"No. I must not. I'm in love with my new wife."

"We will not tell her."

He was no match for her sensuality. In a second, he thrust into her. The passion was so honest that Mei Li sensed very little irritation during the penetration. Her mind was swimming with new-found delight.

"Oh, I am so happy. At last, I am a woman. Don't let it end. It is so beautiful."

But he was helpless and too eager. In a few seconds, the rapid in and out movements catapulted his passion to an ejaculation. His frenzied movements and irregular moaning subsided rapidly. Mei Li wanted more, but it was over in a flash. She barely had time for a groan of ecstasy. She knew about orgasms from self-masturbation, and she had dreamt about experiencing one in her first encounter with sexual intercourse.

She sighed in disappointment.

Her partner jumped up, toweled himself dry, put on his clothes, pressed a fifty dollar bill into Mei Li's hand, and was gone—embarrassed, ashamed, afraid, wondering what he had done to his life, hardly thinking about what he had done to hers.

Mei Li cried as she tidied up the room. Gradually, her frustration disappeared, and her mind focused on the enormous tip she had earned in a few seconds time. The thought flashed through her brain, *Supanee is probably right. With little effort, I can make a lot of money. After I become rich and independent, I'll run away from this kind of life. My sexual longings can wait until then.*

Supanee, who had already collected his share of the twenty dollars for the massage, greeted her in the dim hallway.

"See you tomorrow night?"

"Yes, but I shall sleep in the dormitory tonight. Maybe I'll stay in town for a few nights."

"Good! Now you are being a smart girl."

162

Mei Li never learned about Supanee's journey into the countryside the next morning to visit Tien Chin and Tu Tu. His mission was to insure that Tien Chin would not come to town to bring his daughter home. He gave Tu Tu two-hundred dollars, assuring her that he would take good care of Tien's favorite.

Tien Chin exploded, "We want our daughter back!"

Tu Tu screamed louder, "Shut up! We make twenty dollars all year. We have two-hundred dollars in one day now. There will be one less mouth to feed. Don't be stupid."

Mei Li never saw her mother and father again.

It is estimated that the AIDS rate among prostitutes in Bangkok is seventy percent.

The Way Tom Saw It

I wonder if my friend, Tom Jellineck, has finally gotten it all together. He has almost complete custody of the two kids ("the most important part of my life") after ten years of a rocky marriage. It took some doing in court, and he had to suffer first for three years as a non-custodial parent entitled to but three hours of visitation per week. Debby tried to run away to Boston with the youngsters, but that is all behind him now.

A ruggedly handsome man of fifty-four, medium height, strong face, penetrating brown eyes, black ruffled hair a shade too long around the ears and neck, an athletic body honed by three trips to the gym for weight lifting every week, he seems happy at last. We talked for an hour, and his candor was refreshing. Still, the puzzle does not go away.

"You've been married three times? I'll bet you've had it."

"You know what, Ed? I think I'd try it one more time with Debby. We've been married and divorced twice already." He grinned with that twinkle in his eye.

"Come on, Tom. You must enjoy self-flogging. You said you couldn't stand her heavy addiction to marijuana. You were devastated when she cheated on you after only two years of marriage."

"Look, Ed. When she walked into my store with her mother eleven years ago, I couldn't take my eyes off her. She was that beautiful. In six weeks, we were married. Made no difference that I was eighteen years older. Hell, her current boyfriend is twenty years her senior. Course, I didn't know about the drugs."

"You think marijuana is that bad?"

"Damn right. I could overlook the heavy smoking, the binge

drinking. But I'm almost obsessed about me and my family living a healthy life. I guess I could never convince her to change."

"Geez, Tom. As gorgeous as she sounds, maybe you should have screwed her so much that she would have no time or energy for what you call her drug habit!"

I'm still trying to figure out the pieces. I pondered some cultural differences. He's a Jew. She's an Episcopalian. "No big deal," he adds. She never finished high school. He has an advanced degree in English Lit, teaches at a small college, has a razor-sharp brain, runs the family merchandising business, which he inherited, on the side.

"Debby is smart. Maybe quicker than I am. I just wish we could have worked it out."

"Maybe you're a sucker for beautiful women. Ever try to control your male instincts?"

"You never saw Debby."

Mmm. I better not meet Debby and I better not smoke marijuana with her. I don't need trouble.

"Come on, Tom let's go get a beer."

"Naw, Ed. I don't drink. Let's just go for a walk."

Alex and Max
(A Novella)

It was a special relationship, never making much sense because they were so different.

Alex was—well—almost a rogue, with a flavor for wild-type women, marijuana, J & B by the quart, gin games till the early hours of the morning, expensive cigars, high-stake golf games. His conversation was laced with sarcastic, but friendly, wisecracks. He loved to gamble in the stock market. By profession, he was a lawyer, but it seemed that he worked at it part time.

Max personified Mr. Straight Arrow, the good guy, no cuss words, dedicated to financial achievement, stable home life, a community leader. He wore a friendly countenance, was well liked and respected. Alex figured it out right when he convinced the guys to include him on the annual golf trip to Florida in February. He would be the perfect foil because the wives would never be suspicious of their husbands fooling around with loose women during the vacation as long as Max was part of the group.

Alex and Max met one late afternoon at the Triangle Bar—a watering hole around the corner from the bank—where young lawyers, brokers, bankers, career girls, a hooker or two slunk at the bar or in booths spread around the darkened room to exchange small talk or corny jokes. Alex had suggested the meeting. He explained from his usual lecturing pose, head cocked back, aquiline nose pointing upward, eyes peering downward, cigar in hand, "I want to pick your brains. I hear you are a good market man."

Max accepted the challenge. After all, he was still hustling new accounts. The Triangle Bar did not qualify as his type of hangout, although he would admit that the smoke-filled cozy atmosphere was stimulating to his curiosity about people less conventional than he. Also, he enjoyed looking at the pretty girls who seemed worldly and mysterious, whether they were touchable or not.

The interview went well. Alex was impressed by Max's intellectual credentials: honor graduate from an Ivy League school, former instructor in Accounting at N.Y.U.—alluded to without braggadocio. Max took immediately to this bon vivant, even though shocked by his aggressive behavior toward the stranger sitting next to them at the bar, a girl with a tight skirt above her shapely legs.

"Would you like to spend the evening with me?"

With Alex, everything was up front, no pretenses or apologies for his actions. The girl did not slap his face, but demurely replied, "No."

Then he added, "I've got a hundred dollar bill in my pocket for you."

She laughed, "I don't come that cheap."

The whole scene titillated Max. Perhaps, he liked his new acquaintance because Alex was everything he wasn't. Or maybe he liked him immediately because the attorney quickly made the decision to turn over fifty-thousand dollars to the broker.

"You run the show. I'll give you discretion to do whatever you want. Don't worry if I lose. I'm a big boy. I trust you."

Thus an association was born. A deep friendship eventually developed. Business lunches became frequent, a regular golf game was booked for every Thursday of the summer.

Then, they got lucky. Funny how things happen.

It was a routine luncheon at their city social club. Alex was, as usual, providing the entertainment as he described his latest escapade with a hooker. Max drank it all in, wondering if he would ever have the nerve to stray from his patterned life. His contribution to the conversation centered on investment ideas, boring compared to his new friend's juicy details about exploring the clitoris or exulting in oral sex. When Max mentioned a stock, Syntex, a pharmaceutical company, a doctor friend at the next table, overhearing the word, leaned toward them and smiled.

"Excuse me, but I just happened to hear the name, Syntex. If you like to speculate, buy that stock. The company is about to introduce a birth control pill for men."

Alex's face lit up. Everyone knew that Syntex had a birth control pill for women. But for men?

"Wow, Little Star. (He had a nickname for everyone.) You better get me some of that stock. Maybe a couple of thousand on margin."

"Alex. Come on. Let's check it out first."

"No. I want to take a shot. I feel good about it."

That's the way Alex operated. He was fearless. That was one part of his charm.

The "boys' trip" to Florida that winter featured the spirited camaraderie and normal hell-raising characteristic of all their golf junkets. The daily routine rarely varied: a morning of golf, lunch featuring delicious hamburgers on toasted buns, french fries, catsup, and onions, then the gathering of the eight to ten guys for the afternoon gin ritual in the card room adjacent to the bedrooms.

The setting was raucous—bottles of scotch on a table in the corner, cigar and cigarette smoke blanketing the room, the staccato of loud conversation spiced with expletives erupting from the four card tables, often a scantily clad prostitute wandering around the room, waiting for the next customer to drop his spot in the game to whisk her away into a nearby bedroom for his try at her skills. She would usually end up with a good day's pay from five or six guys, but her presence hardly changed the flow of the gin games.

Max wandered in and out of the action area, partaking in neither the card or sex games. He reveled in being around the action, but was more involved with reading the *Wall Street Journal*, the *New York Times*, or calling his office up north to keep abreast of what was going on in the market. In his scheme of thinking, gin took too much time, diverted too much time from more important activities, such as researching good stocks to buy. As to his participation in the sex party, he most always refrained. Not that he was a goody-goody. But this part of the vacation was more humorous than exciting to him.

"Call the office, Max. See how our Syntex is doing."

It was his way of broadcasting his friend's talent. He had never announced that they had bought the stock for the wrong reason. Syntex had never come up with a birth control pill for men!

In a few seconds, over the din of noise in the room, came the report. "It's up seventeen points today."

With a huge grin on his face and a new cigar pushed in his mouth ready for lighting, he proclaimed, "Well, you bought it for thirty something and now it's six-hundred something. Not bad, Little Star. Keep it up, and I'll end up never having to work again because of you."

With a flourish he peeled off a five-dollar bill from a roll of money, lit it, and put the flame to the cigar. What a friend. What a press agent!

After the Syntex bonanza, Alex trumpeted his broker's knack for picking winners, and Max capitalized on the publicity. His reputation as a sharp money manager was so enticing that he would never again have to solicit new business. He rarely took on a new account because as he said, "If I handle too many people, my efforts will be diluted to the detriment of my loyal clientele."

A mystique grew about his style, his independence: no crybabies or complainers in his client base; all customers must have a minimum of a million dollars in assets under management; all accounts must be discretionary whereby Max had complete authority in all buy and sell decisions. He wore his halo well. He was very good at his craft.

Alex, on the other hand, was content with his stable, but nogrowth law practice. The peaceful afternoons on the golf course or the steamy card games in the afternoon or evening were more important than work. His $150,000 to $200,000 annual income was earned with little effort, and Max chided him for his lack of ambition.

"You are so bright. Your practice would grow if you spent more time at it. What a waste of talent."

"Don't worry about it, Little Star. The way you are making money in the market for me, I don't need more income."

And then, with his classic pontification pose, as if addressing a jury in the courtroom, eyes pointing toward the ceiling in order to enunciate each word carefully for effect, he continued, "I'm living my life the way I want to, enjoying myself. Everything I want, I can afford. I don't have to end up as the richest man in the cemetery."

With his broad, infectious grin, with his arm wrapped around his pal's shoulder, he said, "Too bad you don't have a girlfriend to spice up your life. Then we could really raise hell together!"

It was a drizzly night a few days later when Max was allowed to peer into another part of his confidante's life. They had just finished dinner at their club downtown, happy to be in each other's company, able to talk freely about every topic imaginable from women to golf to stocks to kids and down the list. No secrets were withheld from one another, and each enjoyed the confidence that no sacred words would go beyond their ears.

"Come on, pal. It's time you met my special girl. She's expecting me to drop over, and she'll be glad to see you."

"How do you get away with it? You must spend three or four nights a week over there. Doesn't Rhoda get suspicious?"

"Look, you know our marriage has been dead for years. I don't think she really cares anymore. We no longer match well. Don't forget we got married when she was only seventeen. We have adjusted to our differences. She pretty much does her thing; I do mine. And I don't like her that much. I'm sure she feels the same way about me. Incidentally, don't mention divorce. I'm not interested nor is she."

Max was tingling with anticipation as he followed his pal's

Cadillac to a quiet neighborhood in a wooded area on the outskirts of town. He was curious to meet the girlfriend, the regular, who seemed to get most, but not all, of Alex's passion.

They scurried through the light rain from the parking lot behind the red brick, four-unit, new apartment building into the central hallway. Alex pressed the button in the open foyer, and in a second, the door opened and there stood Elaine—the aloof and darkly forbidding concierge who worked at the downtown Marriott Hotel. Max caught his breath. All he could think of was how many guys had made passes at this once-divorced attractive morsel, who so sweetly had fended off many advances with such finesse. There she was—about five foot six, slim waist, nice hips, firm (it seemed) but not large breasts, jet-black hair surrounding a perfectly symmetrical oval face with warm, dancing eyes. She stepped forward and kissed her man ever so gently on the cheek, beckoned him and his companion into the apartment, slyly whispering, "Alex talks about you all the time. I feel I know you well. It's about time we met."

The dark wood furniture in the living room, the walls decorated with traditional paintings of the great masters—expensive prints—the oriental rugs decorating the floors, the scene greeting Max's eyes said "class," just as did Elaine wearing a dark skirt and light blue silk blouse. Max chuckled inside, delighted for his friend, taken a little back, wondering how in the world he pulled off this coup. Alex was charming, somewhat overweight (not fat) for his six-foot frame, masculine but not pretty, but for whatever reason, you could tell that she adored him. He must have warned her that he was not a good marriage prospect. Obviously, she didn't care, at least on the surface. And obviously, her lifestyle was aided by his generous gifts. As Alex later remarked, they were crazy about each other, so why not treat her like a princess?

After a scotch and some tittering conversation about how shocked some of their associates would be if they were aware of this relationship, Max was off and marveling at the fascinating evening. When he arrived at his home thirty minutes later, he had trouble concealing the cat grin he carried into his living room.

"What's so funny?" His wife smiled.

"Oh, nothing much. Alex always amuses me."

That summer, the Thursday golf game expanded into a full menu of Alex-Max intimacy—lunch, competitive golf involving good players with $100 or so on the line—followed by dinner at a good restaurant downtown, often the Triangle Bar. These were good times for the inseparable pair, particularly after a new perk was added to the package.

Elaine had insisted on preparing dinner for them on Thursday nights. Prime steak on the grill, mashed potatoes, fried onions, plenty of booze and good wine. There was usually classical music in the background; there was the comfort of an oak-paneled den off the living room for after dinner relaxation and conversation. Alex and Max loved their special version of the "boys night out," as most wives in their circle of friends called the Thursday night ritual.

Elaine was such a delight: graceful, efficient, quiet, sexually attractive, witty, at age thirty-one, twelve years younger than Alex. A perfect match for her boyfriend, Max would speculate openly while he engaged in flirtatious chitchat to his pal's good-natured approval. The evening always ended in the den while the hostess tidied up the kitchen and dining room with Max giving his usual lecture.

"What are you waiting for, you dummy? Here's your future, the happiness you can have in your life."

Alex laughed broadly as he sucked on his cigar while contemplating the remarks. "Look, you want me to work hard, you want me to get a divorce and give up a lot of money. You want me to settle down with this girl. Sure, she's great. But I know me. In a couple of years, I'll stray, and I'll be no better off than I am now."

"Maybe yes and maybe no. Right now, your life is dead end. You're crazy to blow this opportunity with Elaine. You'll wake up some day, and she will be gone with a smarter guy than you."

"Aw, let's drop the lecture series and talk about the market or my birdie on the fifth hole yesterday."

In a few minutes, Max was on his way home, thoughts running through his mind about his buddy's rudderless life, wondering how the affair would play out.

Every now and then, Max would wander through the downtown Marriott just to engage the charming concierge standing behind the desk next to the reception counter. Pretending he did not know her, he would strike up a friendly chat.

"Any chance of getting me on a slow boat to China?" asked Max.

"I could probably arrange it."

"Maybe you could come along, and we'd save money if we shared the same room."

"You'd need a vacation after the vacation if we shared the same room!"

Pretty sharp girl, Max would think.

He leaned over the counter and whispered toward her ear, "I'm going to tell Alex that you were trying to turn me on."

The almost inaudible response from the smiling brunette: "Do it. Might do some good if he got a little jealous."

Max whistled quietly under his breath and wondered, *Is there trouble brewing in paradise?*

The days, weeks, months flew by that summer, and the patterns remained much the same. Alex basked in his hedonistic, double life. Max, happy to experience the vicarious thrill of being a part of a secret affair, was an innocent onlooker, almost a peeping Tom with a closed mouth.

Came Labor Day weekend, the end of the golf season, and a change, quite unexpected, took place. The usual foursome was sitting around the table, paying off or collecting on the bets, drinking

173

scotch or vodka, laughing that it was more expensive to win than to lose because the winner always paid for the rounds of libations. Alex's voice, always dominant and lawyerly, was more subdued this time.

"Max, after we shower and you make your usual good husband call to check in at home, let's meet upstairs at the bar for a private chat. There's something on my mind."

Puzzled, Max replied, "Of course. See you in fifteen minutes."

They sat at the far corner of the long, ornate mahogany bar. Joe, a club fixture as bartender for so many years, sporting his signature red bow tie and white shirt, poured the scotch, smiled briefly, and walked to the other end of the empty counter. He had sensed immediately that the guys wanted privacy. There was not the usual laughing and banter characteristic of their imbibing together.

Alex puckered his lips, tapped his glass against his friend's, and muttered, "Cheers," but with no gusto.

"You know you are my closest buddy. I confide in only you. Now get ready for a shock . . . I'm breaking up with Elaine."

Max gasped.

"You're kidding me. You're nuts about her!"

A long silence smothered the tension.

"Look, Max, she's in love with me. But it's not fair to her. She's too good for a bum like me. As long as I'm around, she'll never get what she deserves—a good man, a real partner in life."

They stared at each other for a few seconds more as they sipped their drinks.

"Please, my good friend, don't try to talk me out of it. It took me a long time to make this decision, and it hurts more than anyone could ever imagine. But I think I'm right. And . . . I can't stand the thought of telling her in person. You've got to go over there tonight, without me, have your dinner and explain my decision. I couldn't stand to see her cry. And she will cry."

There was a crack in his voice as he cleared his throat.

"You know. I do think I'm in love with her. But I'll get over it."

This tough, worldly, usually unemotional man was teary-eyed as he glanced vacantly in the opposite direction.

Max leaned over his seat, placed his head on his friend's shoulder, arms around his back.

"Okay. I'll take care of it."

Elaine greeted Max with a warm hug as he entered the living room, which was festively decorated with two Waterford crystal vases containing freshly cut flowers, one vase sitting on the table, the other one on the Chippendale piece next to the Queen Anne chair. A silver bucket loaded with ice surrounding a bottle of Dom Perignon sat on the coffee table. Frank Sinatra's voice was recognizable as the Gershwin number, "Our Love Is Here to Stay," played softly in the background.

"Where's my man? Is he coming later with a surprise gift for our fourth anniversary?"

Elaine looked—well—just luscious. Her black hair was coifed in the latest French twist style, her smile was radiant, her trim figure fit snugly into a navy blue skirt and white silk blouse. The high-heeled shoes emphasized her shapely legs. A stunning sight.

Max smiled awkwardly, hesitated a minute.

"You look positively gorgeous. . . . It will be just the two of us tonight. . . . Alex is not coming. . . . I don't think he'll ever come again."

Elaine, fear in her eyes, seized Max's arm.

"What happened to him? Is he all right?"

"Well. He's okay and he's not okay." Max walked slowly across the room, turned around, and quietly spoke. "He feels he must break up with you."

"Why?" as she held back her tears.

"Because he doesn't want to ruin your life. He won't marry again. He feels there are a lot of good men around who could make you happy. Better men than Alex. As long as he is in your life, you'll never have the chance to find someone for later life as your married mate, someone to bring you happiness in the years ahead. He loves you too much to deprive you of a fuller life."

Elaine sobbed for a couple of minutes, but after two rounds of champagne, she calmed down while she prepared the steak dinner. Tchaikovsky's *Pathetique* was the background music for the two friends as they dined. The conversation was somber. Alex's name was not mentioned. When Elaine kissed him on the cheek and bid him goodnight, Max was fighting to hold back the tears.

Life often takes strange twists, and on this particular autumn evening, fate was kind to Alex, at least in one way. As Max left the apartment and strode toward his car parked in the shadows behind the maple trees, he was startled by the sudden appearance of Rhoda, Alex's wife. She had been hiding behind a row of cars.

"Where's my husband?" she blurted out as she pointed a flash camera in Max's direction. "I know he is here. I've had him tracked by a private detective for the last month. You two eat here every Thursday night."

"I'm not your husband's keeper. I don't know where he is."

"Well, what are you doing here?"

"I'm just making a call on a very good client. We are reviewing her account. Besides, it's none of your business!"

With that, Max glared at Rhoda, who was still brandishing the camera as he swept by her to his car. As he drove away, he was thinking, *What a bitch*. Well, he figured, at least she wouldn't have pictures as evidence against her husband if she were planning a divorce suit to fleece him of tons of money and to keep the three kids away from him in the event of a bitter divorce.

Sleep did not come easily for Max that night. His mind kept racing back and forth about his friend's shattered marriage. Rhoda no longer fit the mold as Alex's partner. She had been attractive as a seventeen-year-old who bedded the young law student in their many passionate moments years ago. The first baby came three months after their marriage. Alex's rationale was that she was good in the sack (his expression), seemed intelligent and fun loving enough, would look good on his arm as his mate when he finished law school and entered the profession, and so came the union. In time, however, the sniping back and forth led to the drifting apart, especially once the sex became routine.

Alex felt justified in his gripes. He cringed when she practiced one-upsmanship to impress their friends. "Oh, Max, anybody can make money in a bull market. With my psychic powers, I could probably be a super stock picker—probably better than you." Or "I could be club champ if I really tried because no one hits it longer than I do."

An avid reader and TV viewer, she had a faculty for remembering minutia and spouting off facts and figures as a show of her intellectual powers. She feigned being an expert on everything including the law—to Alex's chagrin. She rambled all the time about her sixth sense. She had an exaggerated view of her superiority as a golfer, thinker, mind reader, political expert, and card player.

Alex learned to tolerate these annoyances and remained steadfast in his dedication to his three kids and his concept that most marriages involved many irreconcilable differences. He harbored few guilt feelings about his voracious sex appetite, his secret escapades, his enormous capacity to enjoy his things—the golf, the cards, the gambling, the stock market, his reputation as a man's man. Also, he liked money and how important it was in providing him with his idea of the good life.

Max, of course, did not agree with this philosophy, but no matter. He wondered how long they would stick it out. Rhoda was involved with another man, a bachelor, but the affair did not surface for years. No doubt her attempt to catch Alex with Elaine was part of a longer-term strategy to secure better terms in the event of a breakup.

"Fuck her," Alex exploded after Max described the encounter

outside Elaine's apartment the night before. They were standing in the doorway of Alex's office on the nineteenth floor of the Travelers Building. Every detail of the spacious office was a reminder of success. It was situated on the corner—the power location—the two ceiling-sized picture windows at right angles to one another each occupying one wall. The huge cherry wood desk sat forward rectangular fashioned in the open expanse between the windows, with plenty of space for the swivel brown leather chair looking every bit like a throne. Two burgundy leather chairs sat in front of the desk; the matching three-seater sofa, with cherry wood square end tables supporting high brass lamps, occupied the wall next to the entrance.

On the other wall was a collection of neatly framed pictures and mementos. There were the graduation diplomas from the university and the law school, the group photo of the guys on the annual golf trip, a picture of Alex and Max standing next to the golf cart advertising the Doral Country Club, a framed newspaper article of Alex winning the Member-Guest Golf Invitation with his partner from Boston, three individual pictures of the kids, two boys and one girl. The thickly carpeted gray rug added the right feel of conservative elegance. There was a noticeable lack of a bookshelf full of law journals and books. Rhoda's picture was on neither the wall nor his desk. The reek of cigarette and cigar smoke was in the air.

"Now just a minute. Rhoda has every right to be suspicious of you. Her spying doesn't surprise me. But she's bitter, and it looks like she has had it. She's no favorite of mine. How you stuck it out over the years is beyond me. But let's face it. You're no angel. You've been a good father, but a lousy husband. You won't like what I say: you haven't got the guts to get a divorce, and you are too selfish to give up some of your money in a settlement."

Max rarely spoke harshly, and the outburst stunned his comrade. Alex flushed for a second or two, abruptly whirled around, and walked over to look out the window at the street sights below.

He then spoke with measured cadence,

"Yes, you are right. I know it. I'm at the point of not knowing what to do. This I can tell you. From now on, I'm making no pretense of trying to make it work. Rhoda might not be as bad as I make her seem. But the love is gone. We're through, whether we get a divorce or not."

Alex returned to where Max was standing, placed his outstretched arms on his friend's shoulders, and wore a wide grin.

"Come on, pal. Let's go away for a few days together. I need some breathing room, some thinking time. Breaking up with Elaine is tough. The Rhoda mess is tough. We'll play some golf in the Miami area; I'll get me a hooker or two. We'll just relax and enjoy. You need a vacation anyhow. You're working too hard. Some R and R will do you good. I'm sure your sweetie will let you go."

Five days later, they arrived about noon at the Miami International Airport in high spirits. The weather was accommodating— temperature about seventy-seven, lazy, white billowy clouds floating in a sea-blue sky, a gentle breeze fluttering the palm trees scattered outside the terminal building. The snow, slush and bleak skies up north three air hours away were already a distant memory.

Alex was busy doing his thing, tipping generously, five dollars here, ten dollars there, joking with the help, flirting with the receptionist at the hotel, creating the right atmosphere for the start of a great vacation. As the bell captain paused outside the two-bedroom luxury suite, politely awaiting his tip, Alex sauntered over to his side and whispered,

"I'll bet for a fifty-dollar bill, you can give me the telephone number of a beautiful girl who will help me forget all my problems tonight. Must be top quality. No second rate stuff."

"Oh, I can arrange that. How about your buddy?"

"Naw, Max is no good at one-night stands. He's still in love."

The bill was exchanged for the telephone number. The bell captain smiled, "I promise you will not be disappointed."

179

"Okay, Max. We'll get a little lunch, change into our swimsuits, go to the pool for some rays and reading. We look sickly. We need color. Tomorrow, we'll do the golf."

Already, they were about as happy as close friends can be.

Later, at the pool area, Max grabbed Alex's arm.

"Geez, look at that across the pool sunning herself on the lounge chair. She's alone. Let's sit next to her. There's space for two lounges."

"Why not? What's with you?"

"Well, it looks like you will be busy tonight. I might as well try to have a little fun."

"Sweetie wouldn't like it."

"Aw, come on. I probably couldn't even get to first base. But I am in the mood to fool around a bit. Just for kicks."

"Go ahead. I'll never tell."

Casually, they dragged two chairs over to the vacant space next to the attractive girl who fascinated Max.

"Excuse us. Hope you don't mind company."

"Be my guest."

Almost at once, the conversation flowed smoothly. Cindy Friedman was a junior at the University of Miami, majoring in Psychology, enjoying the weekend at the Doral while her mother, a gambling junkie, was over at Paradise Island in the Bahamas for two days, a once-a-month routine for the divorced mother from New York City. Alex wore his quizzical look as Cindy told her stories; Max, ever the naïve one, was a rapt listener. After an hour of friendly small talk, Alex took his leave.

"If I don't get out of this sun, I'll look like a lobster tomorrow. Besides, I've got to take care of some business. You two seem to be hitting it off pretty good. Have fun."

"We will," Cindy rejoined. "And by the way, you ought to check out that cough. It doesn't sound so good."

"Yeah, you're right. I think it's a cold. I'll look after it when I return up north."

Max was almost jubilant as Cindy responded to his earnest flirtation. Her dark good looks, careless smile, perfectly proportioned body stirred his sexual curiosity, and he surprised himself when he ventured, "How would you like to go to dinner tonight with a fellow twice your age?"

"I think you are cute. I'd love it. And Alex said you are a good money manager. I've got some money to invest."

Max was troubled as he dressed for the evening adventure. He fantasized about fucking (a word he used sparingly) Cindy, not just the old in and out that he had experienced a couple of times with hookers on the boys' trip. He pictured the kisses, the caresses, the tender words, the nuzzling against her while dancing, the undressing, the passionate sex. *What the hell is going on with you?* he wondered. *You're married, you love your wife.* Still, the male stirrings would not subside. Cindy looked delicious, and Max was eager to wander.

When Cindy showed no objection to the hand sliding under her skirt and gently squeezing her leg just above the knee during the twenty-minute cab ride to the Eden Roc on the beach, Max marveled at the instant stiffness of his penis.

"Cindy, I can't believe how aroused I feel around you."

"I like that. And I like you, Max. And you are taking me to the Johnny Mathis dinner show? You didn't have to do that. A drink at the Doral Bar would have been just fine."

"Are you kidding? This is a special treat for me. I haven't felt this way in years."

A kiss, a firm clasping of hands and Max was reminiscing about dating the freshman beauty queen back in his college days.

Once they arrived at the posh Eden Roc Hotel, Max swung into action a la Alex style. A generous tip to the cab driver, another one to the doorman, a twenty-dollar bill to the maitre d' who then favored them with a ringside table by the dance floor and entertainment area. Cindy looked radiant, smiling and charming, enjoying the attention she was receiving from Max, who repeatedly reminded her that she could pass for a Hollywood starlet.

The dining room tables were decorated with maroon tablecloths, white napkins, silver candelabra, and cut tropical flowers in a vase adorning each table. The configuration of the room was that of a horseshoe surrounding the dancing area with a few tables on the edges and tiered tables extending back towards the entrance to the room. The seventeen-piece band was playing behind the large dance floor. The waiters were dressed meticulously in black tuxedoes and white bow ties; the sommeliers were colorfully attired with black formal jackets, fire-red brocaded vests and black skintight britches extending down to shining black shoes. The traditional gold chain dropped from around their necks. Sconces with pale yellow bulbs were symmetrically aligned along the white walls enclosing the dining room. Tiny sparkling white bulbs dotted the ceiling above the tables, creating a feeling of dining and dancing under the stars.

The evening flowed romantically with good food, expensive cabernets, tight body-to-body dancing. Johnny Mathis sang his favorite hits, such as "Chances Are" and "My One and Only Love." With the martinis and wine, it was easy for Max to forget all about his wife and kids and think only about his escapade with a sexy young woman.

"Cindy, I reserved for the night a luxury suite. We can have a nightcap and sit around and talk. Maybe you'll tell me the story of your life. Sound okay?"

"Well, you didn't have to go for that extra expense. We could have done the same thing back at the compound."

Max was beaming as they entered the suite—a comfortable sitting room and an adjoining bedroom. Cindy appeared to have a genuine affection for him, and he was confident that she would sleep with him. It would be a storybook conquest—one that would tickle Alex's fancy. His primary concern was whether he could control his passion once they began making love.

They embraced passionately before they sat down on the sofa. Suddenly, Cindy became serious.

"Let's talk a little about the $36,000 I have invested in the bank in CD's. I expect to have more money over a period of a couple of years. Should I put the money in the stock market? I won't need it except for paying my college expenses."

"Well, without knowing your complete situation, I would suggest you diversify into two or three mutual funds. You'll get some growth, and you won't have to follow the market that closely. I'll write down a few names for you to discuss with a reputable broker in your area or perhaps I could handle the transaction for you."

"Good."

With a playful lilt in her voice, she added, "Now Max, I'm going to give you an exciting experience this evening. But I'll charge you only $100—not my usual fee of $200. You've been so nice to me since we met."

They were both giddy from too much wine, and his response carried a humorous tone.

"Well, if you buy the mutual funds through me, I'll waive the normal fees."

They were both laughing as if neither was taking the other one too seriously.

"I'm not joking, Max. Now that we know each other, I can confide in you. You see, I am a professional. I work with a select group of wealthy men. You can become one of my regulars. I must trust that you will help me protect my privacy. I do not want to get involved with any seamy characters."

Max stared in disbelief. The only way he could describe his feelings was "whoosh"—the sucking sound of air escaping from a balloon. Any erotic arousal from two seconds earlier was gone.

Exasperated, he uttered, "Aw, shit."

"Now, Max, don't look so let down. We'll have a nice time . . . I decided a long time ago that the only way I could ever pay my expense for a college education was by working. That's what I'm doing now. When I get my degree, I'll move out to California, find a wealthy businessman who wants a beautiful Jewish girl to show off to his friends, marry him, and live happily ever after. The story about my mom's gambling addiction is a lie. Mother lives in Brooklyn, barely makes a living working at Macy's. My dad walked out on her ten years ago. But she is a survivor, and so am I."

Max's anger subsided. He broke into a hearty laugh.

"And all the time I was thinking that I had swept you off your feet. I should have known better. I've never been a lover boy. I've never had a one-night stand. Why should I succeed now after all these years!"

Max had had plenty of girlfriends in high school and college, had enjoyed various sexual experiences, but for whatever reason, never intercourse. Perhaps it was fear of pregnancy, fear of disease, old-fashioned morality, clumsiness, whatever, coitus did not materialize. He was attractive enough: medium height, athletic build, baby face, coal-black hair, ready smile. There were close calls, especially with girls who regarded him as good husband bait and who schemed that sex was the best way to nail him. When Barb and Max married right after graduation, they were both virgins.

Cindy proceeded as if everything was in order. With her deep-set eyes focused on his, she slowly removed all of her clothing, revealing the considerable allure of her lean body, full breasts, flat stomach, gracefully contoured hips, pubic hair. In short order, she took his clothing off, ignoring his sincere protests.

"I'm limp, Cindy. I lost all desire to make love to you. Let's just go back to the hotel."

"Oh, shush. Stop that nonsense. I can take care of you. Just enjoy."

With a few dexterous movements of her hand on his testicles and penis, with a sharp command, "Put on your rubber. I don't want you to worry about anything."

It took about fifteen to twenty seconds, and it was over. She grinned when he ejaculated so quickly.

"I thought you weren't interested, Max. Now give me the names of two good mutual funds. And by the way, I don't want any money for my service."

When they left the hotel a few minutes later, they looked as happy as two people who had just won the lottery.

Alex was waiting at the room for the arrival of his roommate.

"Well, how did it go?"

Max, shamefaced but amused, related in colorful detail the activities of his evening.

Alex, cigar in hand, smiled.

"Don't feel bad. You were always a good dry-fucker, a good finger-fucker, but never a good fucker. I kinda figured Cindy was a pro. I never bought her story. But what the hell. You had a good time. No harm done. Barb will never find out."

"So, how did your telephone number turn out? Was she great?"

"My good friend, you won't believe this. She was gorgeous. She came to the room, started working on me. Now, are you ready for this? I couldn't get it up. I kept thinking of Elaine. I couldn't even get a good fantasy going. The evening was a complete flop. I'm in bad shape over Elaine."

The friends played a lot of golf the next four days, had no inclination toward women, and cut short the junket by two days. Alex's cough was worse, and he was anxious to consult a doctor. He also wanted to reestablish a relationship with Elaine.

The vacation proved a tonic for Max and his business. Almost immediately, he returned to his skillful approach to picking winners in the market, and he went on a winning roll. His clients were happy. He was at the top of his game.

Alex was running back and forth with medical appointments

185

and tests. The cold was more serious than originally thought.

On his own, Max explored the avenue for reconciliation with Elaine. He stopped by the concierge's desk at the Marriott.

"Alex is unhappy. He misses you. Can I arrange a reunion?"

Elaine responded coolly.

"I did not enjoy being dumped. I'm working on getting rid of the pain. I'll think about seeing him again. In the meantime, I've started dating a guy who has been after me for a couple of years. He's divorced, he's nice, he's the president of a local TV station. Talk to me in a month."

Alex sighed with disappointment when he heard about the conversation with Elaine.

"Well, maybe she found a good one. Let her alone for a while."

A few days later, the two friends were sitting at a far dark corner of the room at the Triangle Bar, sipping scotch, just as they had done when they had first met years earlier. Alex tried to speak cheerfully, but how does a usually strong man put on a happy face when the world has suddenly turned black? When he realizes that his marriage is shot? When he realizes that he has spurned his true love? When he is facing the crisis of his life?

"I talked to the doctor today. All the tests are in. The Xrays show I have the big C. He's putting me in the hospital for treatment."

Max feigned nonchalance even though he had suspected trouble.

"A lot of doctors don't know what the hell they're talking about. Get a second opinion. Even if it is cancer, there are miraculous things going on with new drugs."

"Well, I hope you are right. But advanced lung cancer is not good."

The daily visits to the hospital did little to brighten Alex's spirits. When he showed no interest in the market, in how the guys were playing, in the TV sports events, Max deduced that if his pal were battling, it was a losing battle. He noticed the gradual loss of weight, the powdery pallor of the skin, the deepening creases in the face, the disappearance of the sparkle in the eyes. After a couple of months of ineffective treatments, new experimental medicines were administered, but with no better results. The pain became more intense; it became necessary to increase the dosages of painkillers.

Max suffered with his friend, despaired that he was so helpless. Rhoda made periodic calls with the two younger children. Friends stopped by in a steady procession, but attempts at frivolity were awkward and stilted.

One late afternoon, sitting at the bedside, Max wiped the tears away as he studied the drawn face of his sleeping friend. How could this be, he wondered? This virile man, always overflowing with vitality, gifted with a brilliant mind, blessed with the trappings of success, was literally dying day by day in front of Max's eyes. Alex had everything and now nothing. What goes wrong with a life so full of promise? Would things have been different if he had broken up with Rhoda a few years ago and settled down with Elaine? Did a dissolute lifestyle lead to the breakdown in health? Max, heartbroken, was searching for answers. The prospect of losing his closest companion was devastating.

Alex opened his eyes, delicately reached for Max's hand, and spoke quietly.

"Don't grieve for me, dear friend. I have lived a wonderful life. I would not change it one iota. I have done everything I have wanted to do. I've had more fun and excitement than anyone we know. I've been a lucky guy. I do not want to die. I enjoy life too much. But I know that I am going to die."

"Stop that!"

"And, Little Star, tell Elaine that I love her."

"She wants to see you. Should I bring her over for a visit?"

"No. I don't want her to see me like this."

"Of course, you will watch my family's finances. Rhoda thinks she knows everything. But you'll take care of her the best that you can. Now cheer up. Things aren't that bad."

But they were. Two days later, Alex was gone.

Max was not sure the eulogy and speeches were about Alex. Devoted husband, pillar in the community, hard working, dedicated to his wife. As he glanced around the packed room, he noticed the half-smiles on the faces of the golfing buddies and gin players, the polite nodding by the friends in the legal profession. Were these words about the fun-loving Alex? Probably if it had been up to Alex, he would have preferred a humorist dispensing one-line zingers!

As Barb and Max filed out of the church, he recognized Elaine sitting in the far corner to the rear of the room. She was dabbing her eyes with a hankie.

"Wait a second, Barb. I must have a word with a mutual friend."

She was sitting alone, waiting for Max.

"Hello, Elaine. A bad day." He extended his hand.

"Yes, awful. Would you like to stop over Thursday night? I'll put a couple of steaks on the grill. We can have a good cry together."

"Thanks, dear friend. Good idea. I'll be there."

Alex was gone. The Thursday game could never be the same again: no wisecracks, fewer presses on the golf course, less jocularity around the card table as the bets were paid off and the drinks downed. The "spot"—his spot—was filled immediately. But the spot could never really be filled. There would never be another Alex.

There is an irony to the flow of events in life. Someone is

188

always ready to slip into an empty slot, a reminder that no one is indispensable, that continuity is essential. New players, new expressions, new experiences. After the funeral, in a week or so, Alex became a past memory to most.

Max had conditioned himself for the loss and did not linger on the tragedy. Barb occasionally caught him staring into space, a look of sadness in his eyes. She would grasp his hand in a consoling gesture. These telling moments eventually passed.

"When it's over, it's over. That's it." Those had always been Alex's words—long before the illness. Max had wished otherwise, but was inclined to agree.

"I'll never forget him. I'll always miss him. I can handle it. Life goes on."

In so many cases, the shifting of deep affection from a lost friend to a close soul mate involves a spouse, perhaps a sibling. Barb qualified to fill the gap as a loving, understanding person. In this instance, however, Elaine slid smoothly into the void created by Alex's death. She genuinely liked Max, she too was hurting, she was the strongest link to the past.

"Are you sure we are doing the right thing?"

Elaine's voice suggested tangled emotions when she answered Max's telephone call confirming their date.

"No, I'm not sure. I've been vacillating about this meeting ever since seeing you at the church service. But, let's give it a try."

Max knew he might be venturing onto dangerous ground.

Barb never questioned his having dinner with the boys one night a week. Besides, she looked forward to her evening alone. The kids would be doing their homework in their rooms or hanging out with their closest friends at somebody's home. She would plant herself on the comfortable reclining lounge chair in front of the TV in the recreation room, often falling into a restful sleep. A wife with children and the responsibilities of a busy life needs time for herself for relaxation and renourishing. Too much marital togetherness can become stifling.

What's with this quickened heartbeat, he wondered as he entered the foyer to Elaine's apartment, waiting for her to answer the buzz.

"Hi, Elaine. . . . Wow! Do you look great."

She broke into a huge smile as she accepted the bouquet of red roses thrust into her hands.

"Well, this is a delightful surprise. Thank you. You should have taught Alex better."

"I mostly learned from him. The only person who could probably teach him anything was you," Max grinned.

"No. I mostly learned too. Please sit down while I arrange the flowers in a vase. . . . There now, don't they look beautiful?" She stood back and beamed.

"Now we can have a glass of wine. Healthier than scotch or vodka."

In a moment they were sitting across from each other next to the Kittinger coffee table.

"Good health, better times," he toasted.

"I'll drink to that," she murmured.

Max didn't know quite what to say. They stared at each other awkwardly for a few seconds. He noticed a book on the coffee table, picked it up, and studied the title.

"*Atlas Shrugged*. Ayn Rand. Pretty heavy stuff. I never got around to reading it."

"Oh, it's wonderfully stimulating. She preaches that self-interest makes the world go around. Other things too. Controversial theories. You'd like it."

Max glanced up from the book. "I like you."

"I know that. We better be careful."

"Careful, Elaine. That's my middle name. . . . You know what amazes me? We're not crying."

"I've cried enough lately. I feel better around you. . . . While I prepare our dinner—salmon tonight—better for you than steak, you watch TV and rest. You must have worked hard on the golf course this afternoon."

"If you wouldn't mind, I'd rather listen to Beethoven's *Eroica*. I love that piece. Would you put it on? I can just dream away and meditate."

"Of course."

Max closed his eyes and began to think about where the evening would lead him. Already, Alex's influence was showing. A few years back, Max would never had allowed himself to be in this position. A married man, with two good kids, a devoted wife, secretly enjoying the company of an attractive single woman.

"Better wake up, Little Star."

Max opened his bleary eyes to the tug of her hand on his shoulder. She was standing over him, a smile on her face.

"Glad I won't have to call you Tiger. You've been out for thirty minutes. Dinner is ready. Please sit down."

"How do you know I'm not a tiger?"

"I'm not worried. That's good."

The meal was fine—broiled salmon prepared moistly and underdone, green asparagus, a leafy salad, no bread or butter, a glass of Chablis, fresh strawberries with a touch of cream. Nothing fancy but Max enjoyed the gracious setting, the taste of excellence. He also savored the conversation. Elaine was very bright, able to theorize on many subjects with great insight. For example, when Max suggested during the course of their dinner talk that they should consider reserving Thursday evenings for dining together, she raised her eyebrows as she responded,

"You might be looking for trouble, which you don't need. I'm single, unattached, looking for and needing good company, especially with my man gone forever. You are lucky to have a stable and happy marriage with so many plusses. Why risk jeopardizing your tranquility? We seem to have a good chemistry going. Who knows

191

where that might lead us?"

"Well, you seem to have a solid guy chasing you right now. From where I stand, that relationship looks pretty serious. He will probably end up your lifetime mate in marriage. For the present, we'll be just close friends. You agree that we both want that."

"Indeed yes. But I must confess that as wonderful as he is and as comfortable as I am in his company, he does not turn me on sexually. Nothing like Alex. He handles me as if I were a fine piece of porcelain. I'm earthier than that."

"Oh, in time, you'll become more passionate with him. I assume that you are sleeping with him."

"Yes, but I'm not that excited about that aspect of our relationship. I hope you are right that the sex will improve. He's pretty stiff and proper so far. On the surface, I might look conservative, but underneath, I'm not."

Max flushed. "When you say things like that, I get aroused. You wouldn't want that."

"For now, that's for sure. I'm just warning you for the future."

"Well, I'm a now person. Let's enjoy the present. So, we'll get together once a week just to add a little zest to our lives. We'll become close friends. Good friends are hard to find these days."

"Okay. We'll see how things go."

The Thursday night get-togethers developed into a special treat for the two. The routine varied little with the wine, the meal, the lively give and take of ideas, the background music. The wonder was that in a romantic setting, sexual overtures did not occur during the first three evenings. Max fantasized often about making love to Elaine, but in her presence, he managed to curb his natural desires. Their goodnight kisses were but pecks on the cheek. But how long could he remain so cool while boiling underneath?

The format changed slightly at their fourth rendezvous. (He counted them.) There was little conversation as they sat in the living room after dinner listening to the haunting *Concerto in Blue* by Gershwin with Bernstein on the piano instead of the usual Beethoven fare. They simply stared at each other as they sipped their wine while sitting on the opposite corners of the plush sofa. In thirty minutes, the bottle of wine was finished, the few words between them were muted and inconsequential.

Elaine shifted over closer to her friend, placed her hand behind his neck, gently drew his face toward hers, and placed her lips over his. The kiss was at first quiet, emotional, but when she pressed her tongue between his lips and into his mouth, Max felt the passion of her aggression as she squeezed his head tighter toward her. Her free hand then grasped his hand, led it to her knees and then under her dress and slowly up to her pubic hair guarding her vagina. She was wearing no panties! *How sexy,* he thought. Quickly, his finger slid between her lips. She was receptive and moist, more juicy than he had ever felt Barb or any other woman he had ever known intimately. In a second, he was swimming in ecstasy.

"Now, Max, try to take it easy for a bit. This is about as far as we should go tonight."

Then she searched over his pants to the area of his penis, grabbed it firmly, and squeezed around the hard rod.

"Elaine, I can't handle this. I'm so hot. Hotter than I have been in years."

"Good. I'm not doing badly myself. I want you to fuck me, but not tonight. I might just come from your finger in me. Maybe we should both have an orgasm right now."

With those words, there followed the panting, then simultaneous outbursts of ohs and ahs, the orgasms. Max didn't care that his underwear and pants were getting messy. After a couple of seconds, he sat back contentedly, satisfied and spent, and enjoyed watching Elaine writhe and moan in her passion. She was smiling with her eyes closed.

In a few moments, she opened her eyes, gazing at the subdued Max.

"I guess we were good friends. Now we are going to become lovers too."

Max squirmed nervously. With passion spent, guilt feelings crept into his mind. A woman's excitement does not drop so quickly, so the situation became awkward. Elaine, ever perceptive, sensed the change. She stood up, walked over to the powder room, and returned in five minutes wearing a bright face.

"Tonight was lovely. You do turn me on. I suspected the same. Now you must go home and think about where we go from here. I'm game to get more deeply involved in an affair with you. Your decision is tougher. If you decide to become sexually involved with me, I'll want it twice a week. None of this once a week routine for me. I'll still see my other friend, but you and I will be special. A good way to get started will be for us to meet in New York for a couple of days. You can work out getting away on business. What do you think?"

There was no immediate response. Such hesitation is normal for men in similar circumstances. After ejaculation, wild desire disappears, practical considerations dominate thought process. Max wanted to exit the apartment, to black out the encounter. Pictures of Barb, the kids, his serene home life flooded his brain. He was ashamed of his weakness. Max knew himself, however. He had been secretly wanting an affair to enliven his mundane life. Tomorrow, the guilt trip would be mostly gone. Tomorrow, he would be crazy for Elaine.

"I'm game. Nervous too. I'll set up a business date with a member of Research next Friday morning. We'll meet at the Helmsley Palace on Thursday night. We'll enjoy a suite, have a night on the town. Dinner, a play, the whole works. Can you get away for a night or two?"

"You're on. I'll leave Thursday afternoon, fly down, and return mid-morning Friday. The thought of it excites me. I need getting away."

"Elaine, how in the hell will I be able to stay calm for a week?

And my conscience will be battling me. I know I'm bad. But what the hell. I'm getting older. You're making me feel younger."

"Good. No regrets, I hope. Sounds wonderful."

In no time at all, the week passed.

They stood face to face in the center of the luxurious Helmsley suite, his hands resting on her shoulders, their eyes locked into each other's.

"Now what if I fall in love with you?" she asked.

"Let's not worry about it. Let's just enjoy the evening," he replied.

She walked slowly around the room, drinking in the setting—the billowy yellow curtains falling gracefully from the windows, the French provincial furniture, the gardenias with their luscious fragrance on the coffee table, St. Patrick's Cathedral showing through the picture window.

"I'm not used to this kind of vacation. I might want it all the time."

"Aw, come on. This escapade is a big experiment. We're testing ourselves."

He embraced her, bodies tight together. She backed away.

"Let me change and freshen up. The flight was no fun. I'll be out in a couple of minutes. You make the drinks. I'll have vodka on the rocks."

"Okay. Good idea."

Max was nervous, but excited too. He kept pushing the fleeting visions of Barb and the kids from his mind. He gulped down the scotch to fortify his nerves.

Elaine returned from the powder room fresh and alluring, draped in a terry cloth robe, wearing a pixie smile as she toasted, "To a glorious evening."

They tapped glasses.

"Now," she added. "Close your eyes. Wait a few seconds . . . Now, open them."

Max's eyes feasted on a naked Elaine standing in front of him, her arms spread outward, robe on the floor, her symmetrically proportioned body completely exposed.

"Oh, my God. You are so lovely."

She then stepped forward and kissed him ferociously. After about ten seconds, she broke away.

"Max, I want to feel you in me."

She led him to the edge of the bed, quickly unbelted, and unbuttoned his pants. Then she sat on the edge of the mattress, legs apart and up, grabbed his penis, slid it into her while he was in a standing position.

"The friction is terrific this way. But don't you dare move. I don't want you to come and ruin everything. I might easily come, but I want to be sure you have some juice left for later this evening."

Max was struggling to contain himself.

"I'll hold back as long as you don't move. With you, though, even if I came, I can probably make it again later tonight."

They remained motionless. Max concentrated on thinking of his putting stroke; it was his only way to keep from ejaculating.

"Elaine. I can't stand it. You feel so good."

"You're doing fine. Stay strong."

After a moment of this tantalizing exercise, she whispered, "Now take it out very slowly.

"There. Good going. You were wonderful."

Max, pumped up, but proud of his control, stepped aside to begin dressing.

"I'm ready to explode. I never get this hot with Barb. Never did. What the hell is happening to me?"

"I'm not sure yet. Maybe you've become bored with your marriage, your routine sex life. Or maybe we've found something special between us. An unusual chemistry. I felt it with Alex too. With the right person, I can become very passionate. You might be in trouble because you might believe you are in love with me."

Elaine retired to the powder room, turned around, and poked

her face through the door slightly ajar.

"You are taking me to dinner and a show, aren't you? I better get dressed."

Max, still in an emotional turmoil, but slightly more subdued answered, "We are going to have a time. Let's forget about the future—at least for awhile."

In the elevator down to the lobby, they were laughing like a couple of college kids, exchanging banter.

"Could I pass for a client being entertained? Someone is liable to spot us and start some gossip back home."

"If it's a guy who knows either of us, he'll keep his mouth shut. If it's a gal, well, we might have some trouble. You know, you are a pretty spectacular-looking account."

"Thank you."

"I'll bet you are taking me to a Burger King for a quick bite," she said as they entered the cab.

"Lutece," Max announced to the driver.

"Oh, my. First class all the way?"

"Everything top of the line for my beautiful date."

It was only a few blocks to the restaurant, but the ride through the traffic took fifteen minutes. Elaine was exultant as she kissed Max lightly on the cheek.

"I've always dreamt about eating at Lutece. You make me feel so special."

"You are."

They arrived just in time for their six o'clock reservation. The maitre d' ushered them down the aisle to their side-by-side seats on the right side of the passageway about halfway down on the wall. The tone of Lutece is quiet elegance with its formal white place settings, tuxedoed waiters, subdued conversations. A sampling of canopies was placed on their dishes as they ordered very dry martinis. Max reminded the waiter that they had to catch an eight o'clock curtain time, so their orders were accepted immediately: escargot, rack of lamb, grand marnier soufflé, a fine bottle of burgundy selected by the wine steward. They held hands as they chatted animatedly over their martinis. Max was at his charming best with flattery and funny stories while Elaine never stopped smiling. They were lost in their own private paradise.

Max thought to himself, Y*ou are a rascal. You are cheating on your wife. That's terrible.* The martini soothed his conscience. Elaine was giddy — not loudly — with pleasure.

The talk turned serious as they drank their coffee.

"Max, I don't want to pry. You see, we do so well together. But what's with Barb? Is your marriage falling apart? I don't want to feel like a culprit if you are having problems."

"Well, you are good for me. You spark my interest in sex, which has become pretty humdrum. Funny how I mentioned sex first. Does that mean that I am immature? But there is more to it than that. Barb's life begins and ends each day with the kids. They dominate her thinking, her life. In some ways, I should be grateful. And I am. But there are other things that disturb me. She doesn't enjoy travel, sports, business matters, a host of things I love. I suppose an awful lot of men bump into these marital obstacles — especially between ages forty and fifty. Some of them opt for change — and end up sorry. I meet you, fantasize what could be. It's scary. It's risky. Maybe I'm too much of a romantic, a dreamer. Maybe life isn't supposed to be that proverbial bowl of cherries.

"What about you?"

"Oh, Max, I've been hurt badly twice. My first husband, a handsome, fun-loving moderately successful businessman — he was the chief financial officer for a chain of Wendy's — had some baggage. He drank too much. Not a drunkard, though he hit me a couple of times. He was insanely jealous without reason, he had no interest in music or any culture. Too many verbal battles. I had to leave before it was too late. When I walked out, he was devastated. Then there was Alex. I loved him deeply even though I suspected we would never end up married. I don't even know if it could have worked. Now you come along. A dead end for me? Most likely. I'm ready to settle down with the right man. I do think you and I could be something good together."

"Why do you say that?"

"Well, for one thing, I'd keep you young. And I'd be good for your career. I'm bright and ambitious—just like you. And you are the sexy one. I enjoy adventuresome sex."

"You are the wicked one, Elaine."

"You don't seem to mind."

Max changed the subject. "We have good seats for a great play. Let's get out of here. *West Side Story*."

"Wonderful. You are trying to win my heart?"

The stop and go, kamikaze cab ride across town to the theater was the usual harrowing New York City adventure. They paid scant attention because they were involved in frantic hugging and kissing in the back seat of the cab. During the play, Elaine became teary-eyed as the lovers sang "There's a Place for Us. A Time and Place for Us." They clasped hands tightly. They both fought back tears at the conclusion of the operetta. On the way out, Max laughed, "Do you think somebody spotted us, somebody who recognized us?"

"No. But so what? I'm one of your biggest accounts!"

After battling to grab a cab for ten minutes, Max suggested, "Let's take in Bobby Short at the Carlysle."

"No. I think not. We have to take care of some unfinished business."

"I just hope I can handle you."

"I'm not worried. We'll do fine."

They made love three times that night. Before they went to sleep. In the middle of the night. When they woke up in the morning.

Max was beside himself. "What's going on with me? I'm no longer a kid."

Elaine beamed with pride, "I told you I'd keep you young."

The next Thursday night was all hilarity and wide-mouthed laughter.

"Looks like we dodged the bullet. Nobody saw us in New York," Max ventured.

"We can't be sure," she teased. "You know, the president of the bank has been flirting with me for a month. The last few days he's been more serious. Maybe he heard something. Maybe he thinks he found a live one."

"Yeah, maybe he heard you are a multi-comer."

"Oh, you wise guy." She pushed him gently. "So, where do we go next?"

"How about a cabin in the Adirondacks? I need plenty of rest when you're around."

"No. I prefer Big Sur."

"Not me. I'm rubber-legged looking down from heights."

"Me too. I'm only joking."

"So, what am I eating at Chez Elaine tonight?"

"That's a leading question. But I'll surprise you. Salmon."

"You're getting as bad as me."

For the next several months, that's the way it went. In no time, they became completely familiar with all their likes and dislikes. The similarities were striking: little interest in television, revulsion with overpaid and pampered athletes and rock stars, adulation for Winston Churchill, Art Tatum, the ballet, Leonard Bernstein, Frank Sinatra. It wasn't just the uninhibited sex: it was the non-stop stimulating conversation about fascinating subjects and people. He was annoyed one night when she volunteered that her public boy friend, Jeffrey, the TV executive, was becoming more serious. But he did not feel threatened. Max and Elaine had the right chemistry, were on the same wave length.

"Any problems with Barb or the kids at home?"

"Nope. I felt a little guilty after New York City. But she is so involved with the kids, family, relatives. Sex has become infrequent, unimportant.

" 'We've done all that, it's overrated anyhow!' she often says. She still looks pretty good even though she's put on a few pounds. Quite attractive. She's happy that I have so many activities—the golf, community work, business. As to the kids, they're almost gone. College coming up."

Tornadoes hit with fury when unexpected. Max had settled into a fulfilling relationship for him when the tranquility was pierced.

"We have a problem," Elaine announced one Thursday evening. "Jeffrey is being promoted to a bigger job in Chicago. He wants me to go with him. He asked me to marry him."

Never at a loss for words, Max this time froze for a few seconds in silence.

"What do you want to do?"

"I've thought about it a lot the past couple of days. I'd rather do nothing. But that's a bad decision. There are some gaps in my relationship with Jeffery. But on balance, he would be good for me at this stage of my life. I need some permanence, some stability. Maybe I could settle down for good this time."

"And what about us?"

"I'll put the ball in your court. I'm in love with you. But I can get over it. I got over Alex. If you want to start over again in a new life with me and marry me, I'll join you in a minute. We would be great together. But you'll have to decide. You'd be giving up a lot. Your marriage to a nice lady and all that. You'll have to sort it out. Until you do, neither of us will be sleeping too well."

They did not make love that night. It was a sad evening. Max would have to make one of the biggest decisions of his life within the next seven days. Elaine had promised Jeffery a quick answer.

His head was still throbbing from the distressing turn of events as he entered his house. There was the chattering of many voices in the kitchen. Jammed around the table were Barb, the two kids, five other school friends, all drinking coffee, some smoking, all laughing and enjoying a good old time.

"Did you break eighty today?" came one question. "Have a good day in the market?"

"Sit down and have some coffee. Maybe we'll get you in a Scrabble game."

Barb was the traditional den mother. It was obvious that everybody had tremendous affection for this easygoing regular-gal type of person. There was always warmth accompanying her presence. It was a typical evening at home. Max generally took it for granted, but on this night, it was especially poignant. The talk switched back and forth from dating stories, teachers, sports heroics, applications to colleges, good movies.

After a time, Max stood up.

"See you guys. I've had a busy day. I've got to get ready for tomorrow. Lots going on."

Without missing a beat, the bull session continued unabated.

"Good night."

Max tossed and turned all night. Barb never did show up. She fell asleep as usual on her favorite sofa in the family room long after the gang disappeared with the TV on—the usual occurrence. Three days later, Max phoned Elaine at her desk.

"You're talking to a wreck."

"I'm no bundle of joy myself. Have you made a decision?"

"I'm afraid I haven't got the guts to break up with Barb. This is an awful way to say good-bye. I'm so sad for me, for us. . . . Good luck. I shall never forget you. I shall probably always be in love with you."

After a short silence, Elaine whispered, "You have made a mistake. I hope I am wrong. We shall not meet again. It has been wonderful. Good luck, Max."

The phone clicked off.

There is no need to dwell on what might have been, what should have been. Max lost the spring in his step. The kids went off to college. The couple continued the routine existence. People said they were a happy twosome.

Alex was gone. Elaine was gone. But at least, Max still had Barb, a solid, dependable, borderline-dull presence around the house. Then, quite remarkably, Barb started to change. Completely out of character, she became involved in a gym routine—she who had scoffed the Sunday afternoon football games, who had never read the sports sections in the newspapers, who had laughed that the only thing she ever played was the radio or the TV.

No doubt the barrage of fitness stories in the papers and on television soaked into her mind; the nearness of a Gold's Gym to her favorite supermarket, the cold candor of her bathroom mirror all led her to sign up for a six-month membership at the facility. The time was perfect for change. The children were at college, and in a relatively short period, they would be gone. Barb could at last concentrate on herself, on her marriage, including an improved sexual partnership. The old in and out routine could stand a bit of upgrading. If she shaped up, she might even turn Max on with a new look, a new spirit. Barb was still a beauty at age forty-something with smooth skin, perfect teeth, high cheekbones, warm smile, graceful nose. The slight plumpness should go. Life had been on cruise control. Some shock treatment was in order.

Barb liked her anonymity in the cavernous Gold's Gym complex. There was a variety of people—old, young, male, female, friendly employees, muscular specimens, fat and flabby hopefuls. The equipment was spread out over the vast floor, with treadmills, weights, exercise machines. Barb spent the first hour with an assigned personal trainer who acquainted her with the routines for different machines and instructions on how to proceed in the future on her own. It was exhilarating to be involved in a new activity like an adventure to brighten her life and outlook. She laughed to herself,

"Me straining to get in shape? Barb an athlete? A jock? Come on. But I'll give it a shot."